MIKE ROBERTS

The Reverse Mortgage Revealed

An Industry Insider's Guide to the Reverse Mortgage

This book was professionally typeset on Reedsy.
Find out more at reedsy.com

Dedicated to my Mom and Dad, who I love, respect, and admire.

"Retire from work, but not from life."

— M.K. Soni

Contents

Preface

You've probably seen the TV ads with celebrity spokespeople proclaiming the benefits of a reverse mortgage. Maybe a friend, relative, or colleague got one. Maybe you've heard of reverse mortgages, but thought they were only for broke and desperate people. So what is a reverse mortgage really? How does it really work? Can it truly help seniors live more financially secure in retirement? The purpose of this book is to demystify the reverse mortgage and answer questions like these.

I have over fifteen years of mortgage lending experience and have helped hundreds of seniors get reverse mortgages. I am the first to acknowledge that a reverse mortgage isn't perfect for everybody. However, it can be a fantastic financial solution for the right candidate. For many seniors, a reverse mortgage can even be life changing. Seniors from all walks of life have taken advantage of a reverse mortgage to live a more enjoyable and financially secure retirement.

This book will give you the straight deal about what a reverse mortgage is and how it really works. I'll cut through all the nonsense, misinformation, and hype floating around out there. There's no sales pitches here! You'll get the straightforward inside scoop from an experienced, knowledgeable, and successful industry professional.

By the end of this book, you'll know what a reverse mortgage is and how it works. You'll know who and who shouldn't get a reverse mortgage, what pitfalls to avoid, and what questions to ask. You'll learn about the various payout options and reverse mortgage products available. I'll also teach you insider tips and tricks to expedite the application process, increase proceeds, and reduce closing costs. I've even included case studies based on real-world scenarios that tie together key concepts and terms and demonstrate the ways a reverse mortgage can protect and enhance your retirement lifestyle and financial security.

This book has been crafted with pride and with *you* in mind. My hope is that it helps you make a more informed decision about whether a reverse mortgage is right for you.

Mike Roberts
Founder, MyHECM.com
December 2024

1

Introduction

According to US Census data, the median household net worth for Americans 65 and older is $201,500 [1]. At first blush, that's not a bad statistic. But here's the problem: almost 70% of that number is home equity, which isn't liquid. And if it's not liquid, you can't use it to enhance your retirement lifestyle.

Think about it: if you have no plans to sell your home, it doesn't matter whether you have one dollar or one million dollars worth of home equity. It's just a number on paper. It may be a very *nice* number, but it has no tangible impact on your retirement lifestyle. Case in point: there are seniors with million-dollar free and clear homes in the San Francisco area who practically live on cat food. On paper, they are *millionaires*, yet they barely scrape by on a meager Social Security income.

Yes, home equity is great to have, but it doesn't enhance your retirement lifestyle unless you convert it into *cash*. In the past, there were just two ways to convert home equity into cash: 1) sell your home, or 2) do a "cash out" refinance. Obviously, selling isn't an option if you prefer to stay in your home. A "cash out" refinance can sometimes make sense, but it comes with the downside of a monthly mortgage payment.

Today, there is a third and better option: *the reverse mortgage*. The reverse mortgage enables you to convert home equity into cash *without* selling *or* adding a mortgage payment to your monthly expenses.

The "housing annuity"

In 1969, UCLA professor Yung-Ping Chen testified before Congress about his vision for a "housing annuity". Chen wanted to create a federally-backed reverse mortgage that would enable seniors to "remain in their homes" and "realize the fruits of savings in the form of home equity" [2].

Chen envisioned that the reverse mortgage would work like an annuity, which provides guaranteed retirement income in exchange for an investment. Social Security and pensions are examples of annuities; they offer a guaranteed retirement income in exchange for contributions from you and your employer during your working years. Investment and life insurance companies also offer annuities. You invest a lump sum and they give you a guaranteed income in return. In the case of a reverse mortgage, the "investment" converted (or "annuitized") into income is the equity in your home.

Chen's housing annuity became reality on February 5, 1988, when the Housing and Community Development Act of 1987 was signed into law by President Reagan. The new legislation created a federally-backed reverse mortgage called the *home equity conversion mortgage*, or HECM (commonly pronounced *heck-um* by industry professionals). HECM reverse mortgages are funded by private lenders and insured and regulated by the Federal Housing Administration (FHA) under the authority of the Department of Housing and Urban Development (HUD).

The HECM is not the only reverse mortgage available, but it's by far the most popular. If a friend, family member, or colleague recently got a reverse mortgage, they likely got a HECM. About 30,000 to 50,000 HECMs are written every year in the United States [3].

Many lenders also offer "proprietary" or "jumbo" reverse mortgages, but they're designed for homeowners with home values of $1 million or more. This book focuses exclusively on the HECM, but the information we'll cover should be helpful even if you're considering a jumbo reverse mortgage.

The reverse mortgage stigma

The reverse mortgage is a great product, but it still carries a stigma in the minds of many seniors. Many seniors view the reverse mortgage negatively, so they completely disregard it as a financial option.

In my opinion, the reverse mortgage stigma persists because myths and misconceptions persist. Despite over thirty years of educational efforts by lenders, industry groups, and HUD, people still have a distorted view of how reverse mortgages work. Industry professionals constantly have to cut through the nonsense their clients have heard from well-meaning relatives, friends, advisers, and financial pundits.

Contrary to what you may have heard, the bank does *not* take your house when you get a reverse mortgage. Nor are you selling your house to the bank. A reverse mortgage doesn't strip the equity out of your home or leave a big mess for your heirs to clean up. It's also *not* a loan of last resort just for broke and desperate people.

Yes, many reverse mortgage applicants have limited means and few financial options, but most tend to be at least reasonably financially stable. In fact, many reverse mortgage applicants are even quite wealthy. A few years ago, I did a reverse mortgage for a gentleman with a six-figure income and a seven-figure net worth. Did he really *need* a reverse mortgage? Probably not! But he liked it because it got rid of his mortgage payment, which freed up cash for other things.

A 2019 Brookings Institution study found a significant correlation between accurate information and a positive perception of the reverse mortgage. In other words, when seniors learn how a reverse mortgage really works, *they like it.* According to the study, 85% percent of survey respondents who had a reverse mortgage reported being satisfied or very satisfied with their decision to get one [4].

Obviously, there's a disconnect between perception and reality when it comes to reverse mortgages. As we cover the material to come, I encourage you to disregard the naysayers for now. They mean well, but their opinions are usually based on the same myths and misconceptions you've probably heard as well. My goal is to equip you with *accurate* information so you can decide for yourself if a reverse mortgage is right for you.

2

Features and Basics

The HECM reverse mortgage is a unique mortgage product designed to give you access to your home equity without having to sell your home or take on a mortgage payment.

The minimum qualifying age is 62, but if you're married, only one spouse needs to be at least 62. The younger spouse can qualify as an eligible *non-borrowing spouse (NBS)*, which we'll cover in more detail shortly.

No mortgage payments are required as long as at least one borrower or non-borrowing spouse lives in the home, maintains it, and pays the required *property charges*, which include property taxes, homeowner's insurance, flood insurance, homeowner's association (HOA) dues, ground rents, and special assessments.

You remain the owner of your home and you're free to leave it to your heirs. Your heirs can keep the home by paying off or refinancing the reverse mortgage balance. If your heirs don't want the home, they can sell it, pay off the reverse mortgage, and keep the remaining equity. Your heirs can also let the lender sell the home if they don't want to keep it or hassle with selling it.

A reverse mortgage is best suited for seniors who don't plan to sell, in my opinion, but there are no prepayment penalties or limitations on selling. Selling works the same way as it would for a traditional "forward" mortgage: hire a real estate agent, sell the home, then pay off the reverse mortgage through the proceeds of the sale. The remaining equity in the home goes to you once the reverse mortgage is paid off.

The HECM is a *non recourse* loan, which means the most that will ever have to be repaid is the value of your home. FHA covers the shortage if your home isn't worth enough to settle the entire loan balance.

HECM proceeds are not subject to income taxes and have no impact on Social Security retirement or Medicare benefits. However, the HECM *can* potentially impact Medicaid and Social Security *disability* benefits. If you receive such benefits, make sure you understand how a reverse mortgage could affect them.

The HECM is a mortgage, so it comes with an interest rate like any other mortgage. Most HECMs come with at least some closing costs as well. We'll cover interest rates and closing costs in more detail later.

Flexible and customizable

The HECM offers multiple payout options that can be tailored to your individual financial goals and needs. You can take the proceeds in any of the following ways, which we'll cover in more detail later:

- **Tenure income**: Guaranteed monthly income for life.
- **Term income**: Monthly income for a set dollar amount or time period.
- **Lump sum:** A one-time payout at closing.
- **Line of credit:** A revolving credit line that can be tapped as needed.
- **Any combination of term/tenure, line of credit, and lump sum:** You can mix and match payout options as needed to achieve your financial goals.

You can even restructure the HECM in the future as your financial goals and needs change. All it takes is a quick phone call to your lender and the payment of a $20 administration fee.

Because the HECM comes with multiple payout options, it can accommodate and benefit a variety of financial situations, goals, and needs. Homeowners commonly use the HECM to:

- Eliminate existing mortgage payments.

- Pay off credit cards, medical bills, car loans, and other debts.
- Supplement monthly income.
- Supplement retirement assets.
- Pay for home repairs and improvements.
- Pay for medical expenses or in-home care.
- Set up a safety net to cover long-term care or future unexpected expenses.

If you're at least 62 and have significant equity in your home, it's likely a HECM can benefit you in at least some way.

Protections for non-borrowing spouses

In April 2014, HUD announced new protections for non-borrowing spouses. There are various reasons why an individual might be a non-borrowing spouse, but the most common is age. A spouse who is not yet 62 does not qualify to be a full HECM borrower.

Prior to 2014, it was risky to be a non-borrowing spouse. If the older spouse passed away, it would trigger a *maturity event* that made the HECM balance due and payable in full. A non-borrowing spouse faced with a maturity event had to either refinance or pay off the loan balance in full—or lose the home. Not good, right?

Fortunately, HUD fixed the problem by creating new protections for non-borrowing spouses. Today, non-borrowing spouses can remain living in the home after the older spouse passes away without having to repay the loan balance. This so-called *deferral period* remains in effect as long as the non-borrowing spouse fulfills the program obligations, including living in and maintaining the home and paying the required property charges.

In 2021, HUD expanded deferral period eligibility to include non-borrowing spouses married to individuals who are still living but have resided in a healthcare facility for the last twelve consecutive months.

Also in 2021, HUD removed the requirement for non-borrowing spouses to establish marketable title or demonstrate their legal right to remain in the home following the death of the older spouse. This change made it easier for non-borrowing spouses to establish their eligibility for the deferral period.

Though non-borrowing spouses "inherit" the protections built into the HECM, they do *not* receive any remaining funds in the HECM. Any remaining term/tenure payments are discontinued and/or any available line of credit is closed out when the older spouse passes away.

Insider Tip: *Deferral period eligibility only applies to a non-borrowing spouse you were married to at the time of application. If you get married after getting your reverse mortgage, your new spouse is* not *"grandfathered" into the deferral period protections.*

Common myths and misconceptions

Before we dig into the details of how a HECM works, let's set the record straight on some of the most common myths and misconceptions you may have heard:

- **"I'm giving up ownership of my home."** Not at all. A reverse mortgage is a home loan designed to give you access to home equity without having to sell your home or take on a mortgage payment. You always retain title ownership of your home. The bank is not going on title or buying your home when you get a reverse mortgage.
- **"The reverse mortgage will use up all of my equity."** A reverse mortgage is designed to convert equity into cash, which means it uses up equity over time. However, it's also designed to *preserve* equity. Remember, the HECM is a non recourse loan. FHA covers the shortage if your home isn't worth enough to settle the entire balance. Obviously, FHA can't be constantly covering shortages or the HECM program will become financially unworkable. The HECM is designed to give you access to equity while preserving equity for the future.
- **"I'll leave a big debt to my heirs."** Not at all. Again, the HECM is a non recourse loan. The most that will ever have to be repaid is the value of your home. Any shortage is covered by FHA, which means you won't leave a big debt for your heirs to clean up.

- **"Reverse mortgage interest rates are sky high."** Not at all. In fact, HECM rates are usually comparable to or slightly higher than rates for traditional 30-year fixed "forward" mortgages.
- **"A reverse mortgage is only for broke and desperate people."** Not at all. In fact, broke and desperate people often don't qualify—as we'll cover later. A reverse mortgage is best suited for seniors who are at least somewhat financially stable.
- **"Reverse mortgage closing costs are expensive."** Yes, they can be, *but not always.* We'll cover closing costs and how you can potentially reduce them a little later.
- **"I can't sell my home when I have a reverse mortgage."** Not at all. The HECM is best for homeowners who don't plan to sell anytime soon, but there are no prepayment penalties or limitations on selling.
- **"The lender will get my house in the end."** Not at all. Again, you always remain the owner of your home and you're free to leave it to your heirs. Your heirs will inherit the equity in your home whether they choose to keep it or sell it.
- **"I should get a reverse mortgage only when I really need it."** Definitely not. The best time to get a reverse mortgage is *before* you need it. That way, it's already set to go when you *do* need it. The reverse mortgage is best used as a safety net, *not* a life boat. If you need a financial life boat, your situation may be too dire to qualify. Again, we'll discuss qualifying in more detail later.

When to avoid a reverse mortgage

The HECM reverse mortgage is a great product, but it's not perfect for everybody. There are some scenarios where it probably doesn't make sense to get one. You may want to avoid a reverse mortgage if:

- **You plan to move in the near future.** There are no prepayment penalties or limitations on selling, but a reverse mortgage is best suited for seniors planning to stay in their homes long term. As we'll see later, much of the benefit comes over time. The reverse mortgage also comes with closing costs (which we'll cover in more detail later), so it usually doesn't make sense to incur closing costs if you're not planning to keep the loan for very long.

- **You want to leave the maximum equity possible to your heirs.** The reverse mortgage is designed to convert home equity into cash. This means your loan balance will *increase* and your home equity will *decrease* over time. A reverse mortgage is obviously not a good fit if your goal is to leave the most equity possible to your heirs.
- **You live with children and/or disabled relatives and want them to remain in the home after you pass away.** Remember, the reverse mortgage becomes due and payable in full when the last borrower or non-borrowing spouse passes away. If you have children and/or disabled relatives living with you who are unable to settle the balance after you pass away, it may be best to avoid a reverse mortgage.
- **You know you'll need your home equity in the future.** A reverse mortgage may not make sense if you know you'll need your home equity in the future to move into another home or into a nursing or senior living facility. Again, your loan balance will *increase* over time, which means you'll have less home equity in the future than if you didn't have a reverse mortgage.
- **You lack financial discipline.** A reverse mortgage is probably a bad idea for those who lack financial discipline. Such folks often burn through the proceeds quickly and end up in a worse situation than before they got the reverse mortgage.

3

How a HECM (Really) Works

When people think about a mortgage, they usually have in mind a regular "forward" mortgage like a 30-year or 15-year fixed. This makes sense because so many people have these types of loans. Regular mortgages are simple in concept and most people have a good understanding of how they work: you borrow the money all at once and pay it back in installments over time. Your loan balance *decreases* and your home equity *increases* over time.

The concept of a mortgage in *reverse* is less intuitive, but still pretty simple: you borrow the money over time and pay it back in one lump sum when the loan becomes due and payable. The loan balance *increases* and your home equity *decreases* over time.

A reverse mortgage is basically a negative amortization (or "neg am") loan. Yes, the term "negative amortization" carries a bad connotation—mainly because of the risky pay-option (or "pick-a-pay") loans that were available prior to the 2008 financial crisis. Pay-option loans allowed borrowers to choose from several payment options, including a low minimum payment that didn't cover all of the interest. Any unpaid interest accumulated onto the loan balance, which caused the balance to increase over time.

There's nothing inherently wrong with this kind of loan as long as it's used properly, has some basic safeguards, and there's a complete understanding of how it works. Pay-option loans were originally intended for savvy business owners who wanted additional cash flow management options. Unfortunately, many home buyers were attracted by the low minimum payments and used them to "afford" homes that were otherwise unaffordable.

When home values fell during the Great Recession, many homeowners with pay-option loans found themselves owing far more than their homes were worth. Like most "forward" mortgages, pay-option loans were *full recourse*, which meant the borrower was on the hook for the shortage if the home didn't sell for enough to pay off the entire balance. Many homeowners with pay-option loans ended up tens of thousands of dollars underwater on their mortgages with no means to settle up the shortage.

The HECM is a negative amortization loan as well, but it comes standard with an important safety feature: it's *non recourse*. You, your heirs, and your estate are *not* on the hook for the shortage if your home isn't worth enough to settle the entire loan balance.

How interest is calculated

The HECM is a home loan, so naturally, it comes with an interest rate. HECM rates vary depending on conditions in the financial markets, but they're usually comparable to traditional 30-year fixed mortgage rates.

The note rate on a HECM is called the *initial interest rate (IIR)*. The initial interest rate is an annual rate, but interest accrues monthly—just like a regular "forward" home loan. To see how this works, let's check out an example. Let's assume an initial interest rate of 5% and a loan balance of $100,000 to keep the numbers simple. To calculate interest accruals for a given month, we need to first calculate the monthly interest rate:

```
5% (IIR) / 12 months = 0.41667% (monthly rate)
```

The monthly interest rate is then multiplied by the loan balance to calculate the monthly interest due:

```
0.41667% (monthly rate) * $100,000 (balance) = $416.67 (interest
due)
```

The monthly interest, which equals $416.67 in this example, is calculated exactly the same way as it is for regular "forward" mortgages. The difference, of course, is that you don't have to make payments on the HECM as long as you live in the home and pay the property charges. The unpaid interest is simply added to the loan balance:

```
$100,000 (starting balance) + $416.67 (interest due) = $100,416.67
(new balance)
```

The new loan balance of $100,416.67 is then used to calculate interest accruals for the following month.

Unpaid interest is considered borrowed money, so yes, interest accrues on interest over time. This means the loan balance compounds over time. This isn't a big deal in the early years of the loan when the balance is relatively small, but interest can pile up rapidly in the later years when the balance is much larger. If this concerns you, you can always make occasional payments to reduce the growth of the loan balance over time.

Insider Tip: *Reverse mortgage interest is only tax deductible when it's paid out of your pocket. Some homeowners like to manage both their loan balance and income tax liability by making strategic interest payments on the loan balance. Be sure to consult with a qualified tax professional for information specific to your situation.*

Annual mortgage insurance premium (MIP)

Annual MIP, or *mortgage insurance premium,* also accrues onto the loan balance over time. Annual MIP (along with IMIP, which we'll cover later) helps make the HECM non recourse. FHA uses the money from annual MIP (and IMIP) to cover shortages when HECM loan balances are paid off.

Like interest, MIP accrues on a monthly basis based on an annual percentage rate. FHA periodically changes the MIP rate, but as of publication it is 0.50%. To see how MIP accrues, let's check out an example. To calculate the MIP accruals for the current month, we need to first calculate the monthly MIP rate:

```
0.50% (MIP) / 12 months = 0.041667% (monthly MIP rate)
```

Next, we multiply the monthly rate by the loan balance to get the current MIP due:

```
0.041667% (monthly MIP rate) * $100,000 (balance) = $41.67 (MIP
due)
```

Assuming an initial interest rate of 5.0%, the new loan balance with *both* interest and MIP is calculated as follows:

```
$100,000 (starting balance) + $416.67 (interest due) + $41.67 (MIP
due) = $100,458.34 (new balance)
```

As you can see, the new loan balance with interest and MIP equals $100,458.34. This is the balance on which interest and MIP are calculated for the next month.

How interest and MIP accumulate over time

To see how interest and MIP accumulate over time, let's check out an example. Let's assume a 72-year old homeowner named John wants to pay off his existing mortgage and get rid of his $600 principal and interest payment. John has 26 years left on his mortgage and doesn't plan to sell his home. He figures it makes no sense to keep paying a mortgage he may never pay off anyway. If he can get rid of the mortgage payment, he can spend more money on fun things like fishing, golf, and spending time with his grandchildren.

For this example, let's assume the initial interest rate is fixed at 4.50% and the annual MIP is 0.50%, which means the *total interest rate* is 5.00%. Let's also assume the starting loan balance is $100,000. Figure 1 shows how the loan balance changes over time.

Reverse Mortgage Amortization

Year	Age	MIP	IIR	Loan Balance	Payment Savings
0	72	0.50%	4.50%	$100,000	$7,200
1	73	0.50%	4.50%	$105,116	$7,200
2	74	0.50%	4.50%	$110,494	$7,200
3	75	0.50%	4.50%	$116,147	$7,200
4	76	0.50%	4.50%	$122,090	$7,200
5	77	0.50%	4.50%	$128,336	$7,200
6	78	0.50%	4.50%	$134,902	$7,200
7	79	0.50%	4.50%	$141,804	$7,200
8	80	0.50%	4.50%	$149,059	$7,200
9	81	0.50%	4.50%	$156,685	$7,200
10	82	0.50%	4.50%	$164,701	$7,200
11	83	0.50%	4.50%	$173,127	$7,200
12	84	0.50%	4.50%	$181,985	$7,200
13	85	0.50%	4.50%	$191,296	$7,200
14	86	0.50%	4.50%	$201,083	$7,200
15	87	0.50%	4.50%	$211,370	$7,200
16	88	0.50%	4.50%	$222,185	$7,200
17	89	0.50%	4.50%	$233,552	$7,200
18	90	0.50%	4.50%	$245,501	$7,200
19	91	0.50%	4.50%	$258,061	$7,200
20	92	0.50%	4.50%	$271,264	$7,200

Figure 1. How John's reverse mortgage balance will increase over time due to interest and MIP.

Based on these projections, John's loan balance will grow to $271,264 after 20 years. If that seems a little scary, don't forget that John will also *save* twenty years of mortgage payments. That's a whopping $151,200 he gets to keep in his pocket that would otherwise go to a mortgage he may not live to pay off anyway. That's some serious cash he can spend making great memories with his grandchildren.

Also, don't forget that John is fully protected if the loan balance ever exceeds the value of his home. The HECM is non recourse, which means the most that will ever have to be repaid is the value of the home.

Insider Tip: If you're concerned about the loan balance growth over time, you can always make occasional payments. Even a small interest payment on a monthly basis can substantially reduce the loan balance growth over time.

Servicing fees

Servicing fees are less common today than in the past, but some lenders may still charge them. Servicing fees are usually around $30 per month and are assessed for the life of the loan to cover ongoing customer service expenses. Like interest and MIP, servicing fees do not need to be paid out of pocket; any unpaid servicing fees are simply added to the loan balance. Your lender is required to disclose if they charge a servicing fee.

4

How Lenders Calculate Proceeds

T he HECM is a somewhat complex financial product, so what we'll cover next will also be somewhat complex and technical. My goal is not to overwhelm you with figures and calculations, but I think there is value in covering this material. It will introduce you to important terms and concepts that will help you better understand the estimates and documentation you'll receive from your lender.

The principal limit

The total amount of money available from a HECM reverse mortgage is called the *principal limit (PL)*. Think of the principal limit as the total bag of money available before *mandatory obligations* such as existing mortgages, closing costs, etc., are paid off. To calculate the principal limit, we need to first establish two values: the *maximum claim amount (MCA)* and the *principal limit factor (PLF)*.

Determining the maximum claim amount

The maximum claim amount equals the lesser of the home value or the FHA *lending limit* (also called the *loan limit*). The lending limit for 2025 is $1,209,750.

The maximum claim amount usually equals the home value because most homes are valued less than the lending limit. If the home value is *more* than the lending limit, the maximum claim amount will *equal* the lending limit. For example, if the home is worth $250,000, which is less than the lending limit, the maximum claim amount equals $250,000. If the home is worth $1,500,000, which is *more* than the lending limit, the maximum claim amount *equals* the lending limit. The lending limit effectively caps the home value for purposes of calculating the principal limit.

Note that the lending limit does *not* limit how much a lender can lend or how much you can borrow over time. It simply caps the home value for purposes of calculating the principal limit at the time of application. If your loan balance eventually exceeds the lending limit, *nothing happens.* Your loan is not called due and you're not required to start making mortgage payments.

Determining the principal limit factor

The principal limit factor is derived from a table published by HUD. The lender determines the appropriate principal limit factor based on the age of the youngest borrower (or non-borrowing spouse) and the *expected interest rate (EIR)*.

The expected interest rate is calculated by adding a base *index* rate (currently the 10-Year CMT) and a *margin* set by the lender. For example, if the index is 1.00% and the margin is 2.50%, the expected interest rate equals 3.50%.

It's important to understand that the expected interest rate is *not* the actual note rate on the loan. The note rate (the annual rate at which interest accrues) is the *initial* interest rate. Depending on the HECM product you select (more on that topic later), the expected and initial interest rates could be the same number or they could be different. Regardless, the expected interest rate is used *solely* to determine the principal limit factor, which is then used to calculate the principal limit.

PLFs for a 70-, 80-, and 90-Year Old

EIR	Age 70	Age 80	Age 90
3.00%	0.576	0.642	0.730
3.25%	0.570	0.627	0.720
3.50%	0.554	0.613	0.710
3.75%	0.538	0.599	0.700
4.00%	0.522	0.585	0.691
4.25%	0.507	0.572	0.681
4.50%	0.493	0.559	0.672
4.75%	0.479	0.546	0.662
5.00%	0.465	0.534	0.653
5.25%	0.452	0.522	0.644
5.50%	0.439	0.510	0.636
5.75%	0.427	0.499	0.627
6.00%	0.415	0.488	0.618

Figure 1. Principal limit factors for 70-, 80-, and 90-year old borrowers for a series of expected interest rates.

Figure 1 shows examples of actual principal limit factors for 70-, 80-, and 90-year old borrowers for a series of expected interest rates [5]. You may notice that:

· **Principal limit factors increase with age.** Older borrowers get *higher* principal limit factors, which means they qualify for a larger portion of their home's value than younger borrowers.

· **Principal limit factors *decrease* as the expected interest rate *increases*.** In other words, a *higher* expected interest rate results in a *lower* principal limit factor and reduced proceeds. A *lower* expected interest rate results in a *higher* principal limit factor and *increased* proceeds. This is why the HECM tends to offer more money as interest rates fall and less money as interest rates rise.

Lenders also have some influence over what principal limit factor they use.

Remember, the expected interest rate is calculated by adding an index and a margin *set by the lender.* Lenders have leeway to determine the margin they use, which means they can influence the amount of money you get from a HECM. We'll return to this important point a little later.

Calculating the principal limit

To calculate the principal limit, your lender simply multiplies the maximum claim amount by the principal limit factor. For example, let's assume a home value of $200,000 and a principal limit factor of 0.50. Because the home value is less than the lending limit, the maximum claim amount equals the home value. The principal limit is then calculated as follows:

```
$200,000 (MCA) * 0.50 (PLF) = $100,000 (PL)
```

As you can see, the principal limit factor is basically a loan-to-value percentage determined based on age and expected interest rate. In this example, the principal limit factor is 0.50, or 50% of the home value.

To see how the lending limit applies, let's assume an appraised value of $1,500,000 and the same principal limit factor of 0.50. Because the home value is *higher* than the lending limit, the maximum claim amount equals the lending limit. The principal limit is then calculated as follows:

```
$1,209,750 (MCA) * 0.50 (PLF) = $604,875 (PL)
```

Because the home value is higher than the lending limit, the principal limit equals 50% of the lending limit, *not* the home value. The lending limit effectively caps the home value for purposes of calculating proceeds.

The lending limit is a big reason why many reverse mortgage lenders have introduced so-called "jumbo" reverse mortgages. Jumbo (or "proprietary") reverse mortgages are designed to give homeowners in high cost real estate markets access to more equity than they can get from a HECM because of the lending limit. A detailed discussion of jumbo reverse mortgages is beyond the scope of this book, but you may want to check out a jumbo if you live in a high cost real estate market.

If the calculations we've covered so far are making your head spin, don't worry! Again, you don't need to know how to calculate expected interest rates, look up principal limit factors, and calculate principal limits to be a savvy reverse mortgage shopper. The most important thing to understand is this: you qualify for a *portion* of your home's value based on the expected interest rate and the age of the youngest borrower or non-borrowing spouse. This means that principal limits vary from one borrower to the next because home values, expected interest rates, and ages vary. Principal limits also vary somewhat from one lender to the next because lenders have leeway to select the margin they use to calculate the expected interest rate.

Again, as a rule, principal limit factors tend to increase with age, which means older borrowers qualify for a higher percentage of their home's value than younger borrowers. Principal limit factors also increase as expected interest rates *decrease*. In other words, the HECM tends to offer *more* money when rates are low and *less* money when rates are high.

In my experience, most reverse mortgage borrowers tend to qualify for about 35% to 55% of the maximum claim amount. The percentage can be as high as 70% to 75% for the oldest borrowers during the most favorable interest rate conditions.

Your "walk away" money

Again, the principal limit is the total bag of money available *before* paying the mandatory obligations. Your "walk away" money, which is called the *net principal limit (NPL)*, is the remainder once mandatory obligations are paid. The net principal limit is the portion of the proceeds available for allocation to term/tenure income, lump sum, and line of credit.

To see how lenders calculate the net principal limit, let's check out an example. Let's assume a home value of $300,000 and a mortgage balance of $90,000. Let's also assume, based on age and expected interest rate, that the appropriate principal limit factor is 0.50. Because the home's value is less than the lending limit, the maximum claim amount is equal to $300,000. As before, we first calculate the principal limit as follows:

```
$300,000 (MCA) * 0.50 (PLF) = $150,000 (PL)
```

Let's also assume that, in addition to the mortgage balance of $90,000, there is $1,000 worth of property taxes due and $9,000 worth of closing costs (closing costs will be covered in more detail later). The mandatory obligations are calculated as follows:

```
$90,000 (existing mortgage balance) + $1,000 (property taxes) +
$9,000 (closing costs) = $100,000 (mandatory obligations)
```

Now that we know the total mandatory obligations, we can calculate the net principal limit:

```
$150,000 (PL) - $100,000 (mandatory obligations) = $50,000 (NPL)
```

As you can see, the net principal limit is $50,000. This is the "walk away" money available for allocation to lump sum, line of credit, or term/tenure income. We'll cover each of these payout options in more detail next.

Insider Tip: *You can think of the principal limit like your gross paycheck before deductions are taken out. The net principal limit is the "take home" money after the mandatory obligations (i.e., the "deductions") are paid.*

5

HECM Payout Options

The HECM is a powerful financial tool because it can accomplish many different things. It offers multiple payout options that your lender can customize to meet your individual financial goals and needs. You can take the proceeds as a lump sum, line of credit, monthly term/tenure income, or some combination of all of these options.

Lump sum

A lump sum is a single payout at closing. This option makes sense if you wish to pay off other debt, fund home improvements, or make a large purchase immediately after closing.

Tenure

Tenure offers a lifetime-guaranteed monthly income until the last surviving borrower passes away. Lenders calculate tenure income assuming you'll live to age 99, but it continues even if you live longer or use up all of the equity in your home. Because the tenure plan comes with a lifetime guarantee, the monthly payout is typically lower than what you might get with a term income plan (which we'll cover next).

Term

Term offers monthly income for a set dollar amount or period of time. Term income is almost always higher than tenure income, but it's not guaranteed for life, so it will run out at some point. How soon it runs out depends on how much of a term income you decide to take.

A term plan offers the flexibility to set the payment amount or length of time you want to receive the income. This is helpful if you need extra income temporarily. For example, term income can help hold you over until a new income source (such as Social Security or an annuity) kicks in. Term income can also help pay for health insurance premiums until you're eligible for Medicare.

Line of credit

The line of credit is arguably the best way to take proceeds from a HECM. It's similar to a traditional *home equity line of credit (HELOC)*, but without the potential risks and headaches that come with a HELOC. Here's why I *don't* recommend a HELOC in retirement, despite the well-meaning recommendations of many CPAs, attorneys, and financial advisers:

- **Interest-only payments.** Most HELOCs start with low minimum payments that cover only the interest. Your payment doesn't pay down the balance unless you make extra principal payments.
- **The more you borrow, the bigger your payment.** Your balance can grow rapidly if you use your HELOC to cover large expenses like medical bills, car repairs, or large home maintenance and repair projects. The more you borrow, the bigger your monthly payment.
- **Adjustable rates.** The vast majority of HELOCs come with adjustable rates. If the interest rate increases, your payment will increase as well.
- **HELOCs can be revoked, chopped, or frozen with little notice**. It's risky to use a HELOC as a long-term safety net because you can't rely on it to always be available. If home values fall or credit conditions deteriorate,

your lender may revoke or chop your available credit with little notice, even if you have a perfect payment history and excellent credit. You can't rely on a HELOC to always be available in the future.

- **HELOCs are full recourse.** If home values fall and you owe more than the home is worth, you, your heirs, or your estate will have to pay the shortage to sell the home.
- **The recast.** This is probably the biggest HELOC risk. HELOCs only allow you to borrow during the draw period, which is typically the first ten years of the loan. Once the draw period ends, the bank recasts the loan with a full principal and interest payment that pays back the entire balance over the remaining loan term. This can cause your monthly payment to *double* or *triple*. If you can't afford the new higher payment, you could end up in foreclosure.

The HECM line of credit is a *far* better option for several reasons:

- **No mortgage payments are required.** As long as at least one borrower or non-borrowing spouse lives in the home, maintains it, and pays the property charges, no mortgage payments are required. If you borrow more or rates increase, you *still* never have to make a mortgage payment.
- **The line of credit cannot be taken away.** The line of credit cannot be chopped, revoked, or frozen as long as you meet your program obligations. You can rely on the line of credit to be available when you need it.
- **The HECM is non recourse.** You, your heirs, and your estate will never have to pay out of pocket to settle the loan balance. If your home isn't worth enough to pay off the entire loan balance, FHA will settle the shortage.

Even better, the available line of credit grows larger based on an annual growth rate, giving you access to more equity over time automatically. The line of credit growth rate is always equal to the initial interest rate plus the annual MIP rate. For example, if the initial interest rate is 4.50% and the annual MIP rate is 0.50%, the growth rate is calculated as follows:

```
4.50% (IIR) + 0.50% (MIP) = 5.00% (annual growth rate)
```

If the initial interest rate increases, the line of credit will grow faster, giving you access to more equity faster. Higher rates are usually considered a bad thing, but it can be a very *good* thing if you have a large line of credit.

Like the initial interest rate, growth is based on an *annual* rate, but accrues on a *monthly* basis. This means growth compounds on growth over time. This is why it's a great idea to get a HECM line of credit as early as possible in retirement even if you don't need the money right away. Just get the line of credit set up and let it grow and compound. By the time you actually need the money, you'll likely have far more than if you wait to get a HECM in the future.

To see how the line of credit growth works, let's check out an example. Let's assume a borrower named Allan qualifies for a line of credit that starts off at $150,000 and has a growth rate of 5%. Let's also assume the growth rate doesn't change and Allan doesn't withdraw any additional funds. Figure 3 shows how the available line of credit will grow over time.

Line of Credit Growth

Year	MIP	IIR	Line of Credit
0	0.50%	4.50%	$150,000
1	0.50%	4.50%	$157,674
2	0.50%	4.50%	$165,741
3	0.50%	4.50%	$174,221
4	0.50%	4.50%	$183,134
5	0.50%	4.50%	$192,504
6	0.50%	4.50%	$202,353
7	0.50%	4.50%	$212,705
8	0.50%	4.50%	$223,588
9	0.50%	4.50%	$235,027
10	0.50%	4.50%	$247,051
11	0.50%	4.50%	$259,691
12	0.50%	4.50%	$272,977
13	0.50%	4.50%	$286,943
14	0.50%	4.50%	$301,624
15	0.50%	4.50%	$317,056
16	0.50%	4.50%	$333,277
17	0.50%	4.50%	$350,328
18	0.50%	4.50%	$368,251
19	0.50%	4.50%	$387,092
20	0.50%	4.50%	$406,896

Figure 3. How Allan's line of credit grows over time.

As you can see, the line of credit will grow to $157,674 after just the first year—an increase of $7,674 in a mere twelve months! After five years, the line of credit will be $192,504! If Allan leaves his line of credit untouched for a full 20 years, he'll have almost $407,000 available tax free with just a phone call.

Again, there is no limit on how large the line of credit can grow. Theoretically, it could even grow larger than the value of Allan's home. If that happens, he's beat the system, so to speak. Allan's home value could crash by half over the next 20 years, but he'll still have access to over $400,000 in his line of credit at the 20-year mark. And because the HECM is non recourse, he's not on the hook for any more than the value of the home. Allan has effectively locked in his home equity for his use and protected it against the volatility of the real estate market.

It's probably obvious by now that I'm a big fan of the HECM line of credit. It has all the convenience of a HELOC, but without the potential risks. Best of all, it *grows*. The HECM line of credit essentially turns a portion of your home equity into a liquid and performing retirement asset that automatically increases in value over time. On top of that, it's guaranteed to always be available as long as you meet your program obligations.

Insider Tip: If you choose to make payments on your line of credit, make sure you maintain at least a small balance. If you pay the line of credit to zero, it will close out. Your lender can confirm the minimum balance needed to keep the line of credit open.

"But, I don't need the money right now."

I can't tell you how many times I've heard this from seniors over the years. They put off getting a reverse mortgage because they don't think they need the money right now. If you owe little to nothing on your home and don't need the money right now, *get a reverse mortgage anyway.* You never know when the next financial emergency will strike. The line of credit is a fantastic safety net, but safety nets only work when you have them set up *ahead of time.* It's hard to get insurance when your home is already on fire, right?

If you don't need the money right now, allocate the proceeds to a line of credit and let it grow. There are no interest charges on the untapped credit, so it doesn't hurt you to leave it open and unused. In fact, you're *rewarded* with growth on the unused line of credit. By the time you actually *do* need the money, you'll have substantially more than what you started with.

You'll also likely get far more from growth than you will by waiting to qualify at an older age. Yes, principal limit factors increase with age, but growth gets you a much better return than waiting to qualify when you're older. To prove it, let's look at an example. Let's assume a scenario with an expected interest rate of 4%, age 70, and a home value of $300,000. Based on these parameters and the latest HUD principal limit factor tables, the principal limit is calculated as follows (we'll disregard mandatory obligations for the sake of simplicity):

```
$300,000 (MCA) * 0.522 (PLF) = $156,600 (PL)
```

Now, let's assume the same scenario, but change the age to 80—an increase of ten years. Again, using the latest HUD principal limit factor tables, the principal limit is calculated as follows:

```
$300,000 (MCA) * 0.585 (PLF) = $175,500 (PL)
```

As you can see, the principal limit at age 80 is $18,900 higher than it was at age 70. Pretty nice, right? Or, is it?

Let's see how the numbers look if this borrower instead gets the line of credit at age 70 and sits on it for ten years. Assuming a 4% growth rate, this is how the numbers work out:

```
$156,600 (PL) + 10 Years of 4% Growth = $233,464
```

Wow! This borrower would have a line of credit that is almost $58,000 higher because of growth than he would have by waiting ten years to qualify at an older age.

Folks, as you can see, waiting is not the way to go. If a reverse mortgage makes sense, set one up even if you don't need the money right now. Allocate the proceeds to a line of credit and let it grow and compound. By the time you need it, you'll likely have much more to work with than if you wait.

Modified term/tenure

As you research and shop around for a reverse mortgage, you may run across two additional payout options called *modified term* and *modified tenure*. A modified term or tenure plan is simply a term or tenure plan paired with a line of credit.

Insider Tip: *Though I've used the term "income" in my explanations of the term and tenure payout options, term/tenure plans are typically not considered income for tax purposes. Mortgage proceeds are a loan, so they're not taxed as income. Be sure to consult with a qualified tax professional for information specific to your situation.*

6

HECM Loan Products

There are two main HECM reverse mortgage products available: the *fixed-rate HECM* and the *variable-rate HECM*. Which one makes the most sense for you depends on the available proceeds and your financial goals. We'll cover the basics of each and explain the scenarios where one could make more sense than the other.

The fixed-rate HECM

- **Initial interest rate:** Fixed
- **Payout options:** Lump sum

The fixed-rate HECM offers an interest rate that does not change throughout the life of the loan. However, the rate is typically higher than the initial interest rate for the variable-rate HECM.

The fixed-rate HECM offers only a lump sum payout. All available proceeds *must* be taken as a lump sum at closing, even if you don't need all the money right now. There is no option to take proceeds as a term/tenure plan and/or line of credit.

Unless you're paying off a large mortgage balance, the fixed-rate HECM will typically offer less proceeds than the variable-rate HECM. We'll cover the reasons why shortly.

The variable-rate HECM

- **Initial interest rate:** Variable
- **Payout options:** Any combination of lump sum, term/tenure, or line of credit.

The variable-rate HECM is more popular than the fixed-rate HECM because it's more flexible and usually offers more money. You can take the proceeds as any combination of lump sum, monthly term/tenure plan, or line of credit.

As the name implies, the variable-rate HECM has an initial interest rate that can change over time. The initial interest rate is calculated by adding together an index and a margin. For example, if the index is 2.50% and the margin 2.50%, the fully-indexed initial interest rate is 5.0%. The margin is set by the lender and will never change over the life of the loan. The index, on the other hand, *can* change. If the index increases, the initial interest rate will increase as well, but only within limits called *caps*. *Caps* limit how much the initial interest rate can increase with each rate adjustment and over the life of the loan.

The variable-rate HECM used to be based on the LIBOR index, but the LIBOR has been phased out in favor of the CMT, or *Constant Maturity Treasury* index, and the SOFR, or *Secured Overnight Financing Rate* index. The reverse mortgage industry has used the CMT in the past, so you'll probably encounter it the most when you work with lenders.

You may also encounter a few different variable-rate HECM products that differ in how the initial interest rate is structured and managed over the life of the loan. The following variable-rate products tend to have lower starting initial interest rates, but more frequent rate adjustments:

- **1-Month CMT with a lifetime cap of 5% above the start rate** - The initial interest rate is based on the 1-Month CMT index. The rate adjusts monthly with a lifetime cap of 5% above the start rate.
- **1-Month CMT with a lifetime cap of 10% above the start rate** - The initial interest rate is based on the 1-Month CMT index. The rate adjusts monthly

with a lifetime cap of 10% above the start rate. The initial interest rate on this product will likely start off a little lower than the one above.

The following HECM products tend to have *higher* initial interest rates, but the caps and rate adjustments are more conservative:

- **Annual CMT with a lifetime cap of 5% above the start rate** – The initial interest rate is based on the annual CMT index. The rate adjusts annually with a lifetime cap of 5% above the start rate. This product is very similar to the Annual LIBOR Cap 5 that was popular between 2014 and 2020.
- **Annual CMT with a lifetime cap of 2% above the start rate** – The initial interest rate is based on the annual CMT index. The rate adjusts annually with a lifetime cap of 2% above the start rate. Because this option has a lower lifetime cap, the initial interest rate will likely start off higher than the annual CMT product with the 5% lifetime cap.

You may run across similar products based on the SOFR index, but the CMT-based products will probably be the most common.

It's important to note that the caps are simply a *ceiling* for the initial interest rate. Just because the initial interest rate *can* adjust to a certain rate doesn't mean it actually *will*. If you're nervous about a variable rate, just remember that you're not required to make a mortgage payment as long as you meet your program obligations. The monthly mortgage payment is always *zero* even if the initial interest rate increases in the future.

Also, don't forget that the line of credit growth rate is tied to the initial interest rate. If the initial interest rate increases, the growth rate on your line of credit will increase as well, which means your line of credit will grow faster.

Insider Tip: If you owe little or nothing on your home, are planning to allocate the proceeds to a line of credit, and don't need the money any time soon, consider asking the lender to increase the margin. You may sacrifice some principal limit, but you'll gain a higher growth rate over the long term. The trick is to find the "sweet spot" where you get a higher growth rate without sacrificing too much principal limit in the process. A good lender can help you with this.

The 60% rule

The biggest consideration when deciding between the variable-rate and fixed-rate HECMs will likely be the total proceeds available. Depending on your existing mortgage balance and/or other mandatory obligations, the variable-rate HECM may offer significantly more money because of what I call the 60% *rule*.

FHA implemented the 60% rule in 2014 to discourage borrowers from using up the proceeds too quickly. This rule change also targeted lenders who encouraged borrowers to take all the proceeds at closing even if they didn't need the money right away. Lenders often encouraged full draws because it resulted in a higher starting loan balance that accrued more interest.

The 60% rule works like this: if your mandatory obligations (closing costs, existing mortgages and liens, set-asides, taxes due, etc.) are less than 60% of the principal limit, you can take up to the difference between the mandatory obligations and 60% of the principal limit at closing and/or during the first twelve months of the loan. If the mandatory obligations are *more* than 60% of the principal limit, you can take up to 10% of the principal limit or the difference between the mandatory obligations and the principal limit, whichever is less. Any remaining unavailable portion of the principal limit will be unlocked at the one-year anniversary of the loan, *depending on the HECM product you choose.* Yes, this is a bit complicated, but we'll break it down with some examples in a moment.

Now, this is where a quirk in the HECM comes into play. Remember, the fixed-rate HECM offers only a lump sum payout *at closing.* The fixed-rate HECM does *not* offer any payouts *after* closing. Any principal limit not borrowed at closing from a fixed-rate HECM is essentially forfeited. The variable-rate HECM usually offers more money because payouts are allowed *after* closing (assuming the entire principal limit hasn't already been borrowed). Any principal limit not available at closing via the variable-rate HECM will come available after one year. To see the 60% rule in action, let's check out a few examples.

Example #1: Mandatory obligations are less than 60%

For our first example, let's assume the principal limit is $150,000 and the mandatory obligations are $50,000. Again, if the mandatory obligations are *less* than 60% of the principal limit, the maximum allowed withdrawal at closing is the difference between the mandatory obligations and 60% of the principal limit. To calculate the maximum allowed withdrawal at closing, we need to first calculate 60% of the principal limit:

```
$150,000 (principal limit) * 60% = $90,000
```

As you can see, 60% of the $150,000 principal limit equals $90,000. Because the mandatory obligations are less than 60% of the principal limit, the maximum allowed withdrawal at closing will be the difference between the mandatory obligations and 60% of the principal limit:

```
$90,000 (60% of principal limit) - $50,000 (mandatory obligations)
= $40,000 (max withdrawal at closing)
```

As you can see, this borrower has $40,000 available at closing after covering the $50,000 in mandatory obligations. If the borrower selects the variable-rate HECM, the $40,000 can be taken as any combination of a lump sum, line of credit, or term/tenure income. The remaining 40% of the principal limit, which equals $60,000, will come available automatically a year after closing.

If the borrower chooses the fixed-rate HECM, the entire $40,000 *must* be taken as a lump sum at closing. No additional money will be available in one year.

Example #2: Mandatory obligations are greater than 60%

If the mandatory obligations equal 60% to 90% of the principal limit, the maximum allowed withdrawal at closing equals 10% of the principal limit. To see how this works, let's check out an example. Let's assume the principal limit again equals $150,000, but the mandatory obligations are $100,000. As before, we first calculate 60% of the principal limit:

```
$150,000 (principal limit) * 60% = $90,000 (60% of principal limit)
```

The mandatory obligations of $100,000 are more than the 60% threshold of $90,000, so the maximum allowed withdrawal at closing equals 10% of the principal limit:

```
$150,000 (principal limit) * 10% = $15,000 (max withdrawal at
closing)
```

If the borrower selects the variable-rate HECM, the $15,000 can be allocated to any combination of lump sum, line of credit, or term/tenure income. The remaining portion of the principal limit will come available in a year.

If the borrower selects the fixed-rate HECM, the entire $15,000 must be taken at closing as a lump sum. No additional money will be available in a year.

Example #3: Both HECM products offer the same amount of money

If the mandatory obligations are more than 90% of the principal limit, the total money available from both HECM products may be roughly the same. To see how this works, let's assume the principal limit is again $150,000, but the mandatory obligations are $140,000. Again, let's first calculate 60% of the principal limit:

```
$150,000 (PL) * 60% = $90,000 (60% of PL)
```

The mandatory obligations of $140,000 equal much more than the 60% threshold of $90,000, so the maximum allowed withdrawal at closing equals 10% of the principal limit:

```
$150,000 (principal limit) * 10% = $15,000 (max withdrawal at
closing)
```

But Houston, we have a problem! There's not enough left in the principal limit to pay out $15,000 at closing. If we pay out $15,000, the proceeds will exceed the principal limit by $5,000, which isn't allowed by FHA. Therefore, the maximum allowed withdrawal at closing is $10,000.

If the borrower selects the variable-rate HECM, the $10,000 can be allocated to any combination of lump sum, line of credit, or term/tenure income. There is no remaining principal limit to be unlocked in a year.

If the borrower selects the fixed-rate HECM, the entire $10,000 must be taken at closing as a lump sum. No additional money is available in a year.

Variable or fixed?

Whether you go fixed or variable depends on your financial needs and your comfort level with an adjustable rate. The variable-rate HECM is more popular because it's more flexible and typically offers more money. The variable-rate HECM probably makes more sense if:

- **You definitely want a term/tenure plan and/or line of credit.** The fixed-rate HECM offers only a lump sum payout. If you want a term/tenure plan or line of credit, the variable-rate HECM is the only option.
- **You owe little to nothing on your home.** The variable-rate HECM will likely offer substantially more money if you owe little to nothing on your home.
- **You don't want all the proceeds right now.** The fixed-rate HECM requires

all proceeds to be taken as a lump sum at closing. If you prefer not to take all the proceeds at closing, then the variable-rate HECM makes more sense.

· **You want to maximize proceeds.** Again, the variable-rate HECM usually offers more money. If you want the most money possible, the variable-rate HECM is probably the way to go.

The fixed-rate HECM might make more sense if:

· **You're truly nervous about an adjustable rate.** The reverse mortgage is intended to *alleviate* financial worries, not create new ones. If an adjustable rate truly worries you, go with the fixed-rate HECM.

· **The net proceeds between the variable-rate and fixed-rate HECMs are the same.** If you have a large mortgage balance, the variable and fixed products may offer roughly the same amount of money. If that's the case, and you're concerned about a variable rate, then go with the fixed.

7

Buying a Home With a HECM

ost people know the HECM as a tool to tap into the equity of a home they already own. Relatively few people know that the HECM can also be used to finance a home purchase *with no mortgage payment*. If that sounds crazy, read on! In my opinion, the HECM for purchase is one of the best kept secrets in the mortgage industry.

How it works is very simple: the bank finances a portion of the purchase price and the rest plus closing costs is your *cash to close*. No mortgage payments are required as long as at least one borrower or non-borrowing spouse lives in the home, maintains it, and pays the required property charges.

A purchase HECM is great for buying a home because it offers increased purchasing power and improved monthly cash flow. It also enables you to keep more money in the bank where it can help protect your retirement lifestyle and financial security.

Calculating cash to close

To calculate the cash to close, we need to first calculate the principal limit, which is the maximum amount the bank will finance. The principal limit for a purchase HECM is calculated exactly the same way as a "regular" HECM: the lender determines the appropriate principal limit factor based on the expected interest rate and age of the youngest borrower or non borrowing spouse, then multiplies it by the maximum claim amount (the lesser of the purchase price or lending limit) to determine the principal limit. Your cash to close equals the difference between the principal limit and the purchase price, plus closing costs.

To see this in action, let's check out an example. Let's assume a purchase price of $250,000 and a principal limit factor of 0.55 based on age and expected interest rate. Because the purchase price is less than the lending limit of $1,209,750, the maximum claim amount equals the purchase price. The principal limit is calculated as follows:

```
$250,000 (MCA/purchase price) * 0.55 (PLF) = $137,500 (PL)
```

Note that the principal limit is *not* the cash to close, it's the amount the bank will *finance*. The cash to close is the difference between the principal limit and the purchase price, plus closing costs. Closing costs will be covered in more detail later, but for this example let's assume they're $10,000. The cash to close is calculated as follows:

```
$250,000 (MCA/purchase price) - $137,500 (PL) + $10,000 (closing
costs) = $122,500 (cash to close)
```

As you can see, the cash to close, which includes the down payment and closing costs, is $122,500. The lender finances the rest with no mortgage payment. Pretty cool, eh?

Now, let's look at an example with a more expensive home to see how the lending limit comes into play. For this example, let's assume a purchase price of $1,500,000. Because the purchase price is higher than the lending limit of $1,209,750, the maximum claim amount equals the lending limit. As before, let's assume the principal limit factor is 0.55, so the principal limit calculation is as follows:

```
$1,209,750 (MCA) * 0.55 (PLF) = $665,363 (PL)
```

Again, the principal limit is calculated based on the maximum claim amount, not the purchase price. When the purchase price exceeds the lending limit, the maximum claim amount equals the lending limit. Let's again assume the closing costs are $10,000, which means the cash to close is calculated as follows:

```
$1,500,000 (purchase price) - $665,363 (PL) + $10,000 (closing
costs) = $844,637 (cash to close)
```

As you can see, this buyer's cash to close is $844,637. The rest of the purchase price is financed by the bank with no mortgage payment.

As with a "regular" HECM, principal limits increase with age. Older borrowers qualify for higher principal limits, which means they need less cash to close than younger borrowers.

Principal limits also tend to increase as interest rates *decrease*. In other words, cash to close is usually lower when interest rates are lower.

Increased financial security and purchasing power

The HECM for purchase is a fantastic way to buy a home because it enables you to avoid a mortgage payment (which is great for monthly cash flow) without paying 100% cash for the house. When you buy a home outright with cash, you're investing a huge amount of *liquid* cash in *non* liquid home equity. Remember, home equity is great to have, but it can't be used for anything. It can't be used to fund your retirement lifestyle or pay for unexpected expenses. The HECM for purchase enables you to purchase a home with no mortgage payment and keep more money *in the bank* where it can help protect your retirement lifestyle and financial security.

The HECM for purchase also increases your purchasing power. Normally, if you have only $200,000 to buy a house and want to avoid a mortgage payment, you're limited to buying a home priced at $200,000 or less. But if you can finance roughly half the purchase price (depending on age and interest rate conditions, of course) with no mortgage payment, you can now spend as much as $400,000 on a home. The HECM for purchase significantly increases your purchasing power.

Insider Tip: *If you're purchasing with the variable-rate HECM and have more money on hand than is needed for your down payment and closing costs, you may consider making a large lump sum payment on the loan balance shortly after closing. This recoups line of credit, which will grow over time. Paying down the balance will also reduce interest costs and preserve equity for longer. You will have financed a home purchase without a mortgage payment and turned part of your home's value into a liquid retirement "account" with a guaranteed growth rate. Be sure to check with your lender about how this could work.*

8

Closing Costs

A reverse mortgage is a home loan, so it typically comes with at least some closing costs. How much the costs are depends on the value of your home, where your home is located, and prevailing interest rate conditions. There's no set amount that applies to every HECM loan scenario.

You may have heard that reverse mortgage closing costs are high. In fact, this is one of the most common objections to a reverse mortgage. Yes, the costs *can* be relatively high compared to other mortgage products, *but not always*. Regardless of the amount, you typically do *not* need to pay the closing costs out of pocket. Most lenders will allow you to roll them into the new loan. The exception is HECM for purchase, which we covered in the previous chapter. If you're buying a home with a HECM, you'll need to pay the closing costs out of pocket as part of your cash to close.

Reverse mortgage closing costs typically fall into three categories: *third-party costs*, *origination*, and *IMIP*. Let's cover each category in more detail, then we'll get into some ways to potentially reduce closing costs.

Third-party costs

Third-party costs cover the various third-party services your lender will hire to complete your reverse mortgage. Such services could include title, escrow, appraisal, flood certification, tax certification, HOA certification, attorney's fees, credit report, notary, government recording, and state tax stamps (where applicable). Total third-party costs vary widely depending on the state and loan scenario, but they're usually in the $2,000 to $4,000 range for most people. If you live in a state with tax stamps (such as Florida or Virginia), your third-party costs could be significantly higher.

Insider Tip: You can shop for your own title and escrow, but make sure the company you choose has recently closed reverse mortgages. It's not worth it to try and save a few bucks on title and escrow if the title company creates problems because they don't know what they're doing.

Origination

Origination fees are charged by lenders to cover the costs associated with processing, underwriting, and closing your reverse mortgage. Lenders typically calculate origination fees based on the maximum claim amount.

By law, the most a lender can charge is 2% of the first $200,000 of the maximum claim amount, plus 1% of the maximum claim amount *over* $200,000. The most a lender can charge regardless of maximum claim amount is $6,000. For example, if the maximum claim amount is $200,000, the most the lender can charge is $4,000, or 2% of the first $200,000 worth of maximum claim amount.

If the maximum claim amount is $300,000, the most the lender can charge is $5,000—2% for the first $200,000 (which equals $4,000) plus another 1% of the maximum claim amount *over* $200,000 (which equals another $1,000).

Initial mortgage insurance premium (IMIP)

IMIP, or *initial mortgage insurance premium,* is a one-time fee charged by FHA at closing. Like annual MIP, IMIP premiums go into the FHA mortgage insurance fund to settle up shortages when HECM balances are paid off.

HUD occasionally changes the IMIP amount, but as of this writing it equals 2% of the maximum claim amount. To see how the IMIP calculation works, let's check out some examples.

For the first example, let's assume a home value of $200,000. Because the home value is below the lending limit, the maximum claim amount also equals $200,000. The IMIP calculation works as follows:

```
2% * $200,000 (maximum claim amount) = $4,000 (IMIP)
```

As you can see, 2% of the maximum claim amount equals an IMIP premium of $4,000.

To see how the lending limit applies, let's assume a home value of $1,500,000. The home value is higher than the current lending limit of $1,209,750, so the maximum claim amount equals the lending limit. The IMIP calculation works as follows:

```
2% * $1,209,750 (maximum claim amount) = $24,195 (IMIP)
```

In this example, 2% of the maximum claim amount equals an IMIP premium of $24,195. As you can see, the lending limit effectively caps the IMIP premium. The most that can be charged, regardless of home value, is 2% of the lending limit.

Rates and closing costs are often negotiable

You may be able to negotiate a reduction in rate and/or closing costs, depending on the lender you're working with, interest rate conditions, and your starting loan amount. If you're paying off a large existing mortgage or taking a large lump sum at closing, you may be in a particularly strong negotiating position. Large loan amounts generate more interest for the lender than small loan amounts, so your lender may have the leeway to reduce the rate and/or costs.

On the other hand, if your starting loan amount is small, you may have less negotiating power. For instance, if your home is free and clear and you're allocating all of the proceeds to a line of credit or term/tenure income, the starting loan amount will be small and the lender will likely have little leeway to offer a discount.

Regardless of loan amount, the best way to get a discount is to simply *ask*. Reverse mortgage lenders operate in a highly competitive industry, so they want your business. The worst they can say is *no*, right?

If you successfully negotiate a rate reduction, not only will interest costs be lower, but you may also receive more proceeds. Remember, the principal limit is calculated based on the expected interest rate, which is calculated based on a margin set by the lender. If the lender reduces the margin, it reduces both the initial interest rate and the expected interest rate, which reduces interest costs and increases proceeds.

Lenders offer closing cost discounts in the form of a *lender credit*. Lenders don't waive or remove closing costs, they use a lender credit to *offset* closing costs. For example, if the total closing costs are $10,000 and you receive a lender credit for $8,000, the *net* closing costs charged will be $2,000. The lender will still break down the full $10,000 in closing costs on the appropriate disclosures, but $8,000 of the costs will be paid on your behalf by the lender credit.

You may remember that closing costs are considered a mandatory obligation, which means they're paid out of the principal limit. If closing costs decrease, it should increase the total net proceeds by the same amount.

Insider Tip: If interest rates are really low, your loan may price below the so-called "floor" rate. This means the lender may be able to increase the margin without reducing your principal limit. A higher margin may enable your lender to offer a healthy lender credit to cover closing costs. Having said that, don't forget that a higher margin increases the initial interest rate, which increases interest costs over the life of the loan. A higher margin will also increase the line of credit growth rate.

A few negotiation tips

If you decide to negotiate for a rate or cost reduction, here are some tips that may help:

- As with traditional "forward" mortgages, there's a trade off between interest rate and closing costs. If the lender gives you a large lender credit, don't expect a large rate reduction as well. Lenders are businesses, right? They have to make money somewhere.
- Again, it's much easier for lenders to offer lender credits and/or rate reductions on large starting loan balances. If you're borrowing very little at closing, it's unlikely you'll get a large rate reduction or lender credit.
- Lenders often have more room to negotiate when prevailing interest rates are falling. If prevailing rates are rising, lenders usually have less room to negotiate.
- Remember that the line of credit growth rate is tied to the initial interest rate. A reduction in rate typically means lower interest costs and higher proceeds, but it also means a reduced line of credit growth rate.
- If you already have a HECM and are refinancing for better terms (we'll cover more about HECM refinances later), you may have added negotiating power with your current servicer. Servicers make money by servicing loans, so they don't want to lose loans to other lenders.
- You may have more negotiating power if you have a written offer with better terms from another lender. This is why it can be worthwhile to talk to a few different lenders before moving forward with your reverse mortgage application. We'll cover more about how the application process works and how to shop for a reverse mortgage in later chapters.
- Consider experience, expertise, and professionalism as you shop around as well. Inexperienced lenders and originators often compete solely on fees and rate because they have little else to offer. They may offer the cheapest loan, but they could be a nightmare to work with if they don't know what they're doing. If a cut rate lender is offering a better deal than another lender you'd rather work with, ask your preferred lender to match

the cheaper offer. If they accommodate, you'll be getting the best deal *and* the best service.

Don't forget that your lender has to make money or there's no point for them to write the loan. It doesn't hurt to ask for a rate and/or closing cost reduction, but be reasonable about it. Don't ask for the moon and expect the stars as well.

Insider Tip: If you've selected the variable-rate HECM and plan to allocate all the proceeds to a line of credit, you may consider paying all or part of the closing costs with cash (if you have the means to do so, of course). This increases the size of your starting line of credit and reduces interest costs over time. Just remember to keep a small balance on the line of credit so it doesn't close out. Your lender can confirm the minimum balance needed.

9

Getting a HECM

T he HECM is fundamentally just a home loan, so the process of getting one is similar to that of a regular "forward" home loan. There are six basic steps in the application and approval process:

- Prequalification
- Counseling
- Application
- Appraisal
- Approval
- Closing

The application and approval process typically lasts around sixty days, but it can be shorter for well-qualified applicants. It can also be longer if you have a complex financial profile or if your home needs repairs (more on that later).

Step 1: Prequalification

Finding a lender

The first step is to find a lender and get prequalified. If you don't know who to work with, ask for referrals from friends, colleagues, neighbors, or relatives. The reverse mortgage has increased in popularity in recent years, so there's a good chance you know somebody who has one. A trusted real estate agent, financial adviser, or accountant may also be a good referral source. You can also search the HUD website or MyHECM.com for lenders licensed in your state:

- https://www.hud.gov/program_offices/housing/sfh/hecm/hecmlenders
- https://www.myhecm.com/places/

Keep in mind that the vast majority of lenders that do reverse mortgages only do them occasionally. The HECM has unique guidelines and requirements, so I recommend working with a lender that has a lot of HECM experience. You can determine how many HECMs a lender does by searching for them on the most recent HUD endorsement reports:

- https://apps.hud.gov/pub/chums/f17fvc/hecm.cfm

If the lender you're searching for has few endorsements (or doesn't appear at all), you may consider working with a more experienced lender. I'm not saying they can't get your reverse mortgage done, but their inexperience may create hassles and lengthen the time it takes to process your application.

If you'd like to research a lender's reputation, you can search for them on the Better Business Bureau (BBB) website:

- https://www.bbb.org

The BBB is a good resource, but take the negative reviews with a grain of salt. Dissatisfied or angry people are more likely to write reviews than satisfied people, which means there are probably multiple happy customers for every unhappy one that wrote a review. If a lender has a few complaints here and there, it doesn't automatically mean they're a bad lender. It's impossible to please everybody, especially if the lender does a large volume of business.

Getting prequalified

Once you've found a lender, call them and get prequalified. The licensed representative you'll be working with is called a *reverse mortgage professional, originator,* or *loan officer.* The term *originator* will be used here.

Depending on lender procedures, you may work with your originator over the phone or meet them in person in your home. In the initial consultation, expect your originator to ask questions about your income, expenses, credit, and financial goals. You'll likely need to give permission to run a credit report. A good originator asks questions to understand your financial goals, help you achieve them, and make sure you are likely to qualify. Once your originator completes the initial consultation, he or she can put together a proposal.

When presenting the proposal, your originator should be able to clearly present and explain interest rates, closing costs, and proceeds. Proceeds are calculated based on the estimated market value (not tax value) of your home, so make sure the originator is assuming a *realistic* home value. If you're satisfied with the proposal, you can move on to the next step, which is *counseling.*

Insider Tip: Be sure your originator is assuming a realistic value for your home. Shady originators often inflate home value estimates to "hook" you with numbers that look more attractive than they're likely to be.

Step 2: Counseling

The next step in the process is counseling, which is conducted by a HUD-licensed reverse mortgage counselor. The purpose of counseling is to help ensure that you understand the reverse mortgage and are reasonably competent to make financial decisions.

The counseling usually costs around $125 to $175 and is typically paid out of pocket with a debit or credit card. If you're tight on cash, your lender may be willing to pay the counseling fee with proceeds at closing. The counseling agency may also waive the counseling fee if you have a legitimate financial hardship.

Your lender can provide a list of counselors, but they're not allowed to recommend or nudge you towards a particular agency. You can also search for counselors on the HUD website:

· https://entp.hud.gov/idapp/html/hecm_cnslr_look.cfm

The counseling is typically conducted over the phone, but some counselors may insist on meeting in person. Most counseling sessions last about an hour, but it could be longer or shorter depending on the counselor's procedures and how much you already know about the reverse mortgage.

Once you have a confirmed appointment

Be sure to let your originator know once you have a confirmed counseling appointment. Your originator will need to send you three disclosures before you attend counseling: *Reverse Mortgage Comparison, Total Annual Loan Cost (TALC),* and *Amortization Schedule.*

Reverse Mortgage Comparison

The Reverse Mortgage Comparison is somewhat overly complicated, in my opinion, but it's also the most useful of the three. It contains a breakdown of all the figures for one or more reverse mortgage product options. You'll likely see at least one fixed-rate and variable-rate HECM presented. The lender may also present a jumbo reverse mortgage if they offer one in your state and you live in a real estate market with high home values.

Insider Tip: If you want to determine how knowledgeable and experienced your originator is, ask them to explain the entire Reverse Mortgage Comparison in detail. You'll quickly find out if you're working with a rookie or an experienced professional.

Total Annual Loan Cost (TALC)

The Total Annual Loan Cost (TALC) projects the total loan cost, including interest, MIP, and closing costs, over various time frames as a single percentage rate. The total annual loan cost percentage is typically higher for shorter time frames and lower for longer time frames. This makes sense because the closing costs are paid at closing. The Total Annual Loan Cost shows that the HECM is best used as a long-term solution and becomes more cost effective the longer you have it.

Amortization Schedule

The Amortization Schedule shows how your loan balance and home equity could change over time. This disclosure is useful and informative, but it has some limitations.

If you've chosen the fixed-rate HECM, the loan balance projections will be accurate. The rate is fixed and there's only one payout at closing, so it's easy to project how the loan balance will amortize in the future.

If you've chosen the variable-rate HECM, take the estimates with a grain of salt. Remember, unlike the fixed-rate HECM, the variable-rate HECM offers money now *and* in the future. There's no way to predict with certainty how you will use the loan and how interest rates will change in the future.

The counseling certificate

Once you've successfully completed counseling, you'll be issued a counseling certificate valid for 180 days. Your lender will need a copy of the certificate to continue processing your application. You can either fax or email it to your lender or ask the counselor to send it on your behalf.

Step 3: Application

Once you've completed counseling, the next step is to complete and sign your application. Some lenders may send the application by mail for you to complete, sign, and return. Other lenders may send your originator or a notary to meet with you in person to complete and sign the application. You may also be able to sign your application electronically. Your originator will let you know what to expect.

Your lender will also need some important qualifying documents. Your originator will let you know exactly what is needed, but it will likely include at least some of the following:

- Proof of income (W2s, paystubs, 1099s, award letters for Social Security and pensions, etc.)
- Statements for existing mortgages (if applicable)
- Homeowners insurance declarations page (usually the first page of the policy)
- Homeowner's association (HOA) contact information (if applicable)
- Power of attorney (if applicable)
- Identification (driver's license, state ID, passport, etc.)
- Proof of Social Security Number (1099, Social Security card, or some other official verification of your SSN)

Once your lender receives your signed application and qualifying documents, they'll order your FHA case number, which is a unique 10-digit number assigned to every HECM loan file. Your lender must have the case number before they can move on to the next step.

Step 4: Appraisal

The appraisal is an important part of the application process because it documents the value and condition of your home. The value of your home is important because it's used to calculate proceeds. Condition is important because HUD wants to make sure your home is safe, secure, and marketable. A home in marketable condition is less of a risk to the FHA insurance fund than a home in poor condition.

The appraisal is completed according to FHA requirements by a licensed real estate appraiser. Eligible property types include:

- Single-family homes
- 2-4 unit residential properties
- Condos in FHA-approved complexes
- Manufactured homes built after June 15, 1976 that are on a permanent foundation and haven't been installed or occupied at any other location.

FHA appraisals tend to be more detailed than conventional "forward" mortgage appraisals. It's possible for minor issues like peeling paint, dings in walls, or minor wood rot to be noted in the completed report. Don't worry, a few minor repair issues won't disqualify you. You can complete minor repairs concurrently with the processing of your loan application.

The lender may also allow you to complete minor repairs after closing with a *repair set-aside.* Here's how the repair set-aside works: the lender carves out a small portion of the proceeds and sets it aside until you complete the repairs. Once your lender confirms the repairs are complete, they'll release the funds in the set-aside back to you. Lenders typically allow eight to ten months to complete the repairs, but it's in your best interest to complete them as soon as possible. If the repairs aren't done by the twelve-month mark, HUD authorizes your lender to freeze the available funds in your reverse mortgage until the repairs are complete.

Lender procedures vary, but you'll likely need to pay for at least some of the cost of the appraisal out of pocket. Appraisals typically cost around $600 to $700, but they can be more for large and/or unique properties. If you're tight on cash, your lender may be willing to cover most or all of the appraisal charge with the proceeds of the loan.

The appraiser will contact you to set up an appointment a few days after your lender submits the appraisal order. Expect the appraisal inspection to take about 30 minutes to an hour, depending on the size of your home. Your lender will receive the completed report within 7 to 10 days of the inspection.

Insider Tip: *If your home needs minor repairs for wood rot, peeling paint, torn flooring, etc., it's worth your time to complete the repairs before the appraisal. Completing minor repairs ahead of time will make the application process go smoother and faster. If you had a past roof leak that has since been repaired, make sure you've repainted any ceiling stains as well. Ceiling stains are almost guaranteed to be noted in the appraisal report, which means your lender will require a roof inspection to make sure the roof is sound.*

Step 5: Conditional approval and loan processing

Prior to 2014, there were few credit and income requirements to get a HECM reverse mortgage. Applicants could have zero income and terrible credit and still qualify with no problem. Unfortunately, that contributed to a growing default problem (due to nonpayment of property charges) that resulted in losses for the FHA insurance fund. To address the problem, HUD implemented new lending guidelines called *financial assessment*. Today, HUD requires lenders to qualify applicants based on two financial assessment standards called *financial ability* and *financial willingness*.

Financial ability

The financial ability standard helps lenders determine if you have adequate financial resources to pay your living expenses and required property charges. To meet the financial ability standard, you must have adequate *residual income*. Lenders calculate your residual income by subtracting living expenses such debt payments (excluding mortgage payments eliminated by the reverse mortgage), monthly property charges (property taxes, homeowner's insurance, special assessments, HOA dues, etc.), and utilities (estimated based on your home's square footage) from your total monthly income. Your residual income passes if it meets or exceeds a minimum threshold determined by the region you live in and the number of people living in your home.

If your residual income doesn't meet the required threshold, you may still pass financial ability by documenting one or more *compensating factors*. Valid compensating factors include income from a non-borrowing spouse, overtime, seasonal, bonus, or part-time income, or pension or Social Security income beginning in the next twelve months. The net proceeds available from the reverse mortgage can also be a compensating factor.

If you lack a valid compensating factor or if one or more compensating factors fail to get you to the minimum residual income, the lender may still approve your application with a *life expectancy set aside (LESA)*. We'll discuss the LESA in more detail shortly.

Financial willingness

Lenders evaluate your financial willingness by analyzing your credit and how well you manage your financial obligations. Lenders don't care about credit scores; they're more concerned with payment histories for debt obligations and property charges and the presence of derogatory credit like collections, charge offs, bankruptcies, and foreclosures.

You *don't* need to have perfect credit to pass financial willingness. The credit analysis guidelines are complex and beyond the scope of this book, but you'll likely pass financial willingness as long as you pay your bills at least reasonably well.

If you have major credit issues, you may still qualify by documenting one or more *extenuating circumstances*. An extenuating circumstance is an event beyond your control that led directly to the derogatory credit. Valid extenuating circumstances include loss of income due to the death of a spouse, a major medical issue, lost job, divorce, etc. It's not uncommon for these kinds of circumstances to lead to late payments, collections, charge offs, and bankruptcies. If you can document one or more extenuating circumstances and the underwriter can clearly see the chain of events that led to the derogatory credit, you have a good chance of passing financial willingness even with major credit problems.

If you lack satisfactory credit and one or more valid extenuating circumstances, you may still be approved with a LESA, which we'll cover in more detail next.

Insider Tip: *Extenuating circumstances are somewhat subjective and lender guidelines regarding them can vary. If your extenuating circumstance gets turned down by one lender, you may want to check with another lender to see if they'll approve it.*

Life expectancy set-aside (LESA)

If your application fails financial ability and/or financial willingness and you can't document valid compensating factors or extenuating circumstances, respectively, you may still be approved with a *life expectancy set-aside (LESA)*. The purpose of the LESA is to ensure that applicants with poor credit and/or limited income stay current on their property charges.

Here's how the LESA works: the lender sets aside a portion of the proceeds into a line of credit that is used solely to pay property taxes, homeowner's insurance, and flood insurance (if applicable) for the rest of the expected life span (based on government life expectancy tables) of the youngest borrower or non-borrowing spouse. When payments for property taxes, homeowner's insurance, and flood insurance (where applicable) come due, the lender pays them automatically from the LESA.

The amount of the set aside varies based on age and the cost of the property taxes and homeowner's insurance. If your taxes and insurance are low and/or you're on the older end of the age curve, the LESA will be a relatively low amount. If your taxes and insurance are high and/or you're on the younger end of the age curve, the LESA may consume a large portion of the proceeds.

A LESA can sometimes make a reverse mortgage unworkable. For example, if you have a large existing mortgage balance, there may not be enough money available in the reverse mortgage to pay off the existing mortgage and set up the LESA. In such cases, the reverse mortgage is *short to close*, which means you would need to bring money to closing to pay down your mortgage and make up for the shortfall.

It's important to note that a LESA is not *guaranteed* to pay your property taxes and insurance for the rest of your life. The set aside is calculated using government life expectancy tables, which means it's possible to outlive the LESA. If the funds in the LESA run out, you'll be required to start paying the property taxes and insurance again.

Insider Tip: Don't wait to get a reverse mortgage simply for the sake of waiting or because you don't think you need the money right now. A reverse mortgage is best used as a safety net, which works best when you set it up ahead of time. If you wait until you really, really need the money, your credit and/or financial profile may have deteriorated to the point where it may be difficult to qualify. The best time to get a reverse mortgage is when your qualifications are strong and you don't really need the money yet.

Conditional approval

The underwriter will issue a conditional approval once they've analyzed your application and determined that it meets the HECM underwriting requirements. This doesn't mean your loan is complete, however. The approval will likely have at least a few conditions that need to be met before your loan can close. Such conditions could include additional signed disclosures, updated qualifying documents, mortgage payoffs, repairs, etc.

If the appraiser noted major health, safety, marketability, or structural issues with your home, such as a leaky roof, bad foundation, mold, water in the basement, etc., it's likely that the underwriter will require the problems to be fixed *before* your loan can close. Minor repairs like peeling paint or minor wood rot can often be completed after closing with a repair set-aside.

Loan processing

If you're working with a large lender, a processor will typically step into the picture once the underwriter issues the conditional approval. The processor's job is to help complete the outstanding conditions requested by the underwriter. If you're working with a small lender or broker, the originator may handle the processing. Regardless, your processor and/or originator may need to involve you to complete some of the approval conditions.

The time frame from conditional approval to closing could be either days or weeks. Clean files with minimal approval conditions often close just days after approval. Complex files with numerous outstanding conditions usually take longer.

Insider Tip: Most reverse mortgage applicants are eager to close at this point in the process, so it can be frustrating when the processor and/or originator calls asking for additional paperwork to satisfy the approval conditions. Be patient with them! They're motivated to finish your loan, too. The HECM is a highly regulated product and there are many, many guidelines for the lender to comply with. The sooner you get the processor and/or originator what they need, the sooner they can close your loan.

Step 6: Closing

The underwriter will issue a final approval and clear your loan for closing once all of the approval conditions are received. Your originator will contact you to go over the final figures and schedule a closing appointment.

Non-purchase transactions come with a three-day rescission or "cooling off" period after closing in which you can rescind the transaction with no questions asked. There is no rescission period for purchase transactions.

Once the three-day rescission period is complete (if applicable), the lender releases funds to escrow. Escrow pays the mandatory obligations and sends you any cash you requested at closing.

Insider Tip: *Escrow will distribute cash at closing in the form of a check or electronic deposit. I recommend choosing an electronic deposit because it's faster and more secure. Your originator can explain how to set it up.*

10

How to Shop For a HECM

The HECM is a complex product with numerous moving parts, which means the written proposals lenders provide are also complex. If you don't know what you're looking for, it can be difficult to determine which of several loan offers is the best.

Fortunately, because the HECM is regulated by HUD, proceeds are calculated in exactly the same way regardless of the lender you're working with. How lenders disclose the figures is fairly consistent as well. We'll cover how to compare loan offers so you can quickly and easily determine which offer is best.

A few items to gather up

Before we proceed, you'll want to gather up a few items:

1. Pen or pencil
2. Calculator
3. Loan Offer Comparison Sheet - This is what we'll use to compile the loan offers so you can easily compare them. You can download the Loan Offer Comparison Sheet from: https://www.myhecm.com/reports/loan-offer-comparison-sheet.pdf

What we'll focus on

When comparing offers, it's important to focus on the figures related to *cost* and *net proceeds*. It doesn't matter how much of a tenure payment you can get, how much cash is available at closing, or how big your line of credit will be in one year. It doesn't matter *how* the bag of money is divided up; what matters is how *big* the bag of money is and how much it *costs* to borrow it.

Having said that, keep in mind that a reverse mortgage offer is more than just the numbers. You don't want to shop based on rates and fees alone. The professionalism, experience, and expertise of the lender also matters. Many mortgage lenders do reverse mortgages, but relatively few have a lot of reverse mortgage experience. Inexperienced lenders often cut their rates and fees to the bone because that's all they have to offer. On paper, it looks like you're getting a great deal, but the application process could be slow and frustrating because the lender doesn't know what they're doing.

Getting loan offers

I recommend comparing offers from no more than three lenders. HECM lending guidelines and calculations are fairly standard across the reverse mortgage industry, so it's probably unnecessary to shop more than three. Refer to the previous chapter for tips on finding good lenders to work with.

Once you've found three lenders, call each to prequalify and get a *Reverse Mortgage Comparison*. The *Reverse Mortgage Comparison* is the best document for comparing offers because it contains all the pertinent figures, including interest rate, closing costs, and the net cash available after paying closing costs. Figure 1, below, shows a sample *Reverse Mortgage Comparison* disclosure.

Reverse Mortgage Comparison

From: Oswald Originator, Reverse Mortgage, Inc.
123 Main Street
Anywhere, USA 00000

Rates and Fees	Libor 1	Libor 2
Index	1YrLibor	1MoLibo
Margin	1.50%	1.50%
Initial Interest Rate	3.29%	2.79%
Expected Interest Rate	2.48%	2.48%
Mortgage Insurance Rate	0.50%	0.50%
Cap on Interest Rate	8.29%	12.79%
Monthly Servicing Fee	$0	
Initial Credit Line Growth Rate	3.29%	2.79%
Calculation		
Home Value	$420,000.00	$420,000.0
Maximum Claim Amount	$420,000.00	$420,000.
Principal Limit	$222,600.00	$222,60(
- Servicing Set Aside	$0.00	$(
Available Principal Limit	$222,600.00	$222,600
- Mortgage Insurance Premium	$8,400.00	$8,400.(
- Origination Fee	$4,200.00	$4,200
- Other Costs	$2,800.00	$2,800
+ Credits	$5,000.00	$5,000.
Max Cash Available	$212,200.00	$212,200.(
- Tax & Insurance Set Aside	$0.00	$0.
Available Funds		
Available Funds	$212,200.00	$212,200
Or Available Monthly Tenure	$780.00	$780.
Requested Payments		
Cash Request	NA	N
Monthly Income Request	NA	N
LOC Re~		

Figure 1. A sample Reverse Mortgage Comparison disclosure with the pertinent information highlighted. This disclosure can look slightly different and use slightly different terminology from one lender to the next.

The *Reverse Mortgage Comparison* is designed to disclose multiple loan options in columns side by side. Most lenders offer the fixed-rate HECM and at least one variable-rate HECM, so you will likely see at least two loan products presented. Some lenders also offer a jumbo proprietary reverse mortgage, so you may see that presented as well. The option currently selected for you by the lender is presented down the center of the page.

You'll notice that a few of the labels in Figure 1 are outlined. These are the numbers we're after to determine which offer is best. The rest of the information isn't relevant for our purposes here. Again, we just want to know how big the bag of money is and how much it's going to cost to borrow it.

Note that the *Reverse Mortgage Comparison* may look slightly different and utilize slightly different terminology that what you see in Figure 1. Ask your originator for help if you're having trouble finding the items needed to complete the *Loan Offer Comparison Sheet* (which we'll go over next).

Completing the Loan Offer Comparison Sheet

Once you have three offers in writing, it's time to compile the most important information onto the *Loan Offer Comparison Sheet*. This sheet is designed to help you easily compare offers side by side. The following is an explanation of each field:

- **Lender name** - The name of the lender you're working with.
- **Originator name** - The name of the originator you're working with.
- **Phone number** - Your originator's direct phone number.
- **Professionalism, experience, and expertise** - On a scale of 1 to 10, with 10 being best, how would you rate your experience working with this lender? How knowledgeable, professional, and competent was the originator? Circle the appropriate number.
- **Variable or fixed** - The HECM comes with two product options, the variable-rate HECM and the fixed-rate HECM. Make sure you're *only* comparing variable-rate offers or fixed-rate offers, not some combination of the two. Circle the appropriate loan product.
- **Maximum claim amount** – This is determined by the value of your home and is used to calculate proceeds. Make sure all the lenders you're shopping with are assuming the same home value.
- **Initial interest rate** – This is the actual note rate on the loan. The *initial interest rate* is calculated by adding an *index* set by the financial markets and a *margin* set by the lender. The lender has some discretion to determine what margin to use. The margin impacts both the initial interest rate and the *expected interest rate*, which is used to calculate

65

proceeds. If the margin is lower, the initial and expected interest rates will be lower and proceeds typically higher. If the margin is higher, the initial and expected interest rates will be higher and the proceeds typically lower. The initial interest rate may also be called the *initial rate*.

- **Principal limit** – This is the gross proceeds available *before* paying off mortgages, closing costs, etc. The principal limit is calculated based on the age of the youngest borrower (or non-borrowing spouse), expected interest rate, and the maximum claim amount.

- **Initial mortgage insurance premium** – This is FHA's upfront mortgage insurance premium. This is a closing cost and is disclosed along with the other closing costs as a dollar amount. This may also be called *mortgage insurance premium, IMIP, or MIP*. Don't get this mixed up with the annual mortgage insurance premium (MIP), which is calculated as an annual percentage rate along with the initial interest rate. We're not concerned about the annual MIP because it's the same for all HECMs regardless of the lender you're working with.

- **Origination** – This is a closing cost charged by the lender to cover their overhead. The most a lender can charge is 2% of the first $200,000 worth of maximum claim amount and 1% of any maximum claim amount over that. The most the lender can charge is $6,000, regardless of maximum claim amount.

- **Other costs** – This covers the third-party services needed to complete your loan, including appraisal, title, escrow, credit report, etc. This is also called *third-party fees* or *third-party costs*. These costs will probably be similar from one lender to the next.

- **Lender credit** – Lenders don't typically waive or eliminate closing costs, they *offset* them using a *lender credit*. A lender credit is essentially a payment to you for purposes of paying all or part of your closing costs. For example, if your closing costs are $5,000 and the lender credit is $4,000, your net closing costs are $1,000.

- **Net principal limit** - This is bottom line amount of money available after paying closing costs.

Note that we're not taking into account existing mortgage balances or set asides in these numbers. We're also not taking into account payout options such as lump sum, line of credit, term/tenure income, etc. Again, the idea is to boil down the numbers to just rate, costs, and the net money available after paying the costs.

Now that we've covered what the various fields mean, let's begin filling in the information for each offer on the *Loan Offer Comparison Sheet.*

Step 1: Fill in the lender information and rating

- Lender name
- Originator name
- Phone number
- Rate the professionalism, experience, and expertise of the lender/originator

Step 2: Fill in the loan offer information

Again, the currently selected loan option is presented down the *middle* of the *Reverse Mortgage Comparison.* It's the loan closest to the labels on the left side of the page. Make sure you pull your figures from this loan option. Fill in the following fields on the *Loan Offer Comparison Sheet* for each lender's offer:

- Variable or fixed (if you're not sure if the loan offer is variable or fixed, ask your originator)
- Maximum claim amount
- Initial interest rate (this may also be called the *initial rate).*
- Principal limit
- Initial mortgage insurance premium (this may also be called *IMIP* or *mortgage insurance premium* and will be a dollar amount, *not* a percentage rate)
- Origination (this may also be called the *origination fee*)
- Other costs (this may also be called *third-party costs* or *3rd-party costs*)

· Lender credit (this may also be called *credits*, *lender credits*, or *other credits*)

If you have difficulty finding these items on the *Reverse Mortgage Comparison* disclosure, ask your originator for help. A good originator should have no problem explaining the *Reverse Mortgage Comparison* in detail. If your originator can't, make sure you revise your rating for professionalism, experience, and expertise accordingly.

Again, it's super important to make sure all offers are assuming the same home value. Home value has a direct impact on proceeds. It will be difficult to compare loan offers if each lender is assuming a different home value.

Step 3: Calculate the net principal limit

Once you've filled in the figures, it's time to calculate the net principal limit, which is the net cash available after paying the closing costs. This is the cash available to you to pay off your mortgage and/or allocate to lump sum, line of credit, term/tenure income, etc.

Use the following formula to calculate the net principal limit for each loan offer:

```
Principal limit - Initial mortgage insurance premium (IMIP) -
Origination - Other costs + Lender credit = Net principal limit
```

The net principal limit is often disclosed as a separate line item on the *Reverse Mortgage Comparison*. It's labeled "Remaining Principal Limit" in Figure 1, but some lenders may label it differently.

Comparing the offers

Once you've calculated the net principal limit for all three offers, it should be clear which lender is offering the most money for the lowest cost. The offer with the highest net principal limit is the best offer—at least as far as the numbers go. Again, a reverse mortgage offer isn't just about the proceeds.

Make sure to take into account the professionalism, experience, and expertise of each lender as well.

If you have a favorite lender, but they don't have the best offer, ask them to match the best offer. Lenders are eager to earn your business. Your favorite lender may be willing to match (or even beat) the best offer, which means you'll get the best lender *and* the best offer. If they're not willing to match, you'll have to decide if the added costs and/or lower payout is worth it to work with them. If they're at least *close* to the best offer, it's probably worth it to move forward with them, in my opinion.

11

After Your HECM Is Complete

Reverse mortgage servicing

Once your reverse mortgage is complete, it is transferred to *servicing*. The job of a servicer is to handle ongoing account maintenance throughout the life of your reverse mortgage. The servicer handles borrower inquiries and requests for funds, monitors property charge payments, distributes LESA payments (if applicable), and facilitates the settling of your loan when it becomes due and payable. The servicer also handles numerous other unseen tasks to ensure compliance with HUD and FHA requirements.

Only the largest lenders are able to service loans. If you closed your reverse mortgage with a large lender, it's possible the same lender will handle servicing. If you closed with a small lender or broker, your reverse mortgage will likely be transferred to a large servicer.

Within a few weeks of the completion of your reverse mortgage, you'll receive a welcome packet with your servicer's contact information. You can contact your servicer at any time to request funds, ask questions, and restructure your payout options. You'll also begin receiving monthly statements with a complete breakdown of your loan balance, interest rate, and funds available.

Insider Tip: Be sure to include your servicer's contact information in your will or trust documents so your executor/heirs know how to reach them.

Annual occupancy check

Remember, HUD requires that you live in your home to keep your reverse mortgage in good standing. Your servicer will mail out an occupancy check form every year asking you to certify that the home is still your primary residence. It's important to return this form promptly (usually within 30 days) or the servicer may assume you're no longer living in the home, which could trigger a maturity event and make the loan due and payable.

In late 2023, HUD updated their requirements to allow for verbal occupancy checks. Instead of filling out and returning a form, you can now complete your occupancy check by phone.

Though you're required to live in your home, it doesn't mean you can't be away for long periods. It's okay to take long trips or travel south for the winter as long as you live in your home for the majority of the year. You're allowed to be away from your home for up to twelve months for medical reasons. Make sure to let your servicer know if you plan to be away from your home for more than two months.

If you have a repair set-aside

If you closed your reverse mortgage with a repair set-aside, make sure you promptly complete the required repairs and let your servicer know once they're done. Once your servicer confirms the completion of the repairs, they'll release the funds in the set-aside back to you. If the repairs aren't completed within 12 months, HUD authorizes your servicer to freeze any available proceeds in your reverse mortgage until the repairs are completed.

If you have a LESA

If you closed your reverse mortgage with a LESA, your servicer will handle paying your property taxes, homeowner's insurance, and flood insurance (if applicable) on your behalf.

Remember, your lender calculated the LESA to last the rest of your life based on government life-expectancy tables. However, there's no way your lender can guarantee that. It's possible the LESA could run out sooner than expected if your property taxes or homeowner's insurance increase more than expected. If your LESA runs out, you'll be responsible for paying the property taxes and homeowner's insurance again.

Refinancing your reverse mortgage

It's possible to refinance a HECM into a new HECM to take advantage of better loan terms. A HECM refinance can make sense if:

- Property values have increased
- Interest rates have decreased
- The FHA lending limit has increased
- Principal limit factors have increased

You can also do a HECM refinance to include a new spouse on a reverse mortgage or change from a variable-rate HECM to a fixed-rate HECM.

The HECM refinance application process is essentially the same as that of a "regular" HECM, but you may not need to attend counseling again if the following three conditions are met:

1. You have received the HECM Anti-Churning Disclosure from the lender you're refinancing with.
2. The increase in the principal limit exceeds the total cost of the HECM refinance by at least five times.
3. Your current HECM closed no more than five years ago.

You may also be eligible for a discount on the IMIP for the new HECM if it's been no more than a few years since you got your current HECM. Be sure to ask your lender about any applicable IMIP discounts.

If you refinance through your current HECM lender, you may also be eligible for additional discounts on the initial interest rate and/or closing costs.

How the HECM balance is settled

Note that the following applies to HECM reverse mortgages with case numbers issued August 4, 2014 or after. There may be variations in the treatment of HECMs originated before August 4, 2014 (mainly with regard to non-borrowing spouses).

Once the servicer learns that all borrowers and/or non-borrowing spouses have passed away, it will issue a Due and Payable notice to the heirs. The servicer may order an appraisal to determine the current market value of the home. The heirs can also request an appraisal of their own at their own expense.

The heirs will have a few options to settle the reverse mortgage balance:

1. **Pay the lesser of the loan balance or 95% of the appraised value to keep the home.** The heirs can settle the loan balance by refinancing or using other assets such as savings or life insurance proceeds.
2. **Sell the property, repay the balance, and keep the remaining equity.** The sales process works just like it would for any other type of mortgage. The heirs hire a real estate agent (or sell it themselves), sell the house, pay off the loan balance at closing, and keep the remaining equity.
3. **Give the lender a Deed in Lieu of foreclosure**. The heirs sign the deed over to the servicer and the servicer sells the property and repays the loan balance.
4. **Do nothing.** The lender uses the foreclosure process to sell the property and repay the loan balance.

The lender is required by HUD to begin foreclosure proceedings if the heirs do not repay the balance in response to the Due and Payable Notice. Proceedings must begin within 90 days, but no sooner than 30 days after the Due and Payable Notice is issued.

I've heard and read conflicting information about the initial time window the heirs have to settle the loan balance and keep the property. Some sources say the initial time window is 90 days. Others say six months. The ambiguity probably means servicers have some flexibility here. It may be safe to assume that the heirs have as much as six months to repay the loan and keep the property.

Of course, keep in mind that the servicer is required to start foreclosure by the 90-day mark. If the foreclosure process moves quickly, it's possible it could be completed before six months have passed. It's in the best interests of the heirs to repay the loan balance as soon as possible if they intend to keep the home. It's also in the best interests of the heirs to be in regular communication with the servicer about their intentions.

If the heirs plan to sell the home, they have an initial time window of six months to complete the sale. If they need more time, they can request up to two 90-day extensions. HUD requires the servicer to foreclose if the home is still not sold at the end of one year.

It's important to understand that the heirs do *not* lose out simply because the servicer begins foreclosure proceedings. HUD requires servicers to *begin* foreclosure by a certain date, but it doesn't mean foreclosure is a done deal. The heirs still have the option to pay off or refinance the loan balance or sell the home.

A normal part of settling reverse mortgages

Most people react negatively to the word "foreclosure"—which makes perfect sense. After all, foreclosure is usually associated with missed payments, hard times, and families losing their homes. However, when you strip out the emotional connotations, "foreclosure" simply refers to the sale of a home by a mortgage lender to repay a mortgage balance. This is true of "forward" mortgages *and* reverse mortgages.

In the reverse mortgage world, foreclosure is a *normal* part of settling up loan balances. A foreclosure doesn't necessarily mean that a reverse mortgage borrower fell on hard times and failed to meet their loan obligations. Many reverse mortgage borrowers have no heirs. Or if they do, the heirs often don't want the home and don't want to mess with selling it. In such cases, the lender pays off the loan via the foreclosure process.

12

Case Studies

Case study #1: Eliminating a big mortgage payment and a whole lot of worry

Mrs. Miller is a 75-year old widow struggling to make ends meet. She and her husband had a good combined income and lived a comfortable (if modest) lifestyle, but he passed away five years ago and took his income with him. Today, Mrs. Miller lives on a meager Social Security check that doesn't even cover all of her monthly expenses.

Figure 1, below, summarizes Mrs. Miller's current cash flow situation, which clearly isn't good. As you can see, her expenses are almost $1,100 more than her income.

Case Studies

Income and Expenses

Income	Expenses	Cash Flow
$1,540	-$2,622	-$1,082

Figure 1. Mrs. Miller's monthly income, expenses, and cash flow.

Mrs. Miller is running negative every month mainly because of her mortgage payment, which is $1,127.33 for the principal and interest. The Millers originally planned to have the house paid off many years ago, but college and wedding expenses for the kids forced them to retire with a mortgage. The mortgage payment wasn't so bad when Mr. Miller was alive and there were two incomes to work with. Today, however, it's a huge financial burden that consumes almost two thirds of Mrs. Miller's income.

Mrs. Miller has managed so far by supplementing her income with monthly withdrawals of $1,100 from her savings. She had substantial savings when her husband died, but her savings account has since dwindled to about $50,000. That's still a lot of money, but with a lot of years left on the mortgage and a good chance she'll live into her eighties, it's obvious her savings won't last as long as she'll need. She needs to improve her cash flow situation fast.

Mrs. Miller considered taking a part-time job to make extra money, but recent health issues have made that unrealistic. She could ask the kids for help, but they have families and financial burdens of their own. She doesn't want to burden them even more. Besides, she wants to remain financially independent; she doesn't want to rely on somebody else for her financial well being.

Before we go further, let's review Mrs. Miller's balance sheet. As you can see in Figure 2, her car is paid off and she has no credit card debt. Her only debt is her mortgage, which has a balance of $184,685 and will be paid off in twenty-three years.

Balance Sheet and Net Worth

Assets	Asset Value	Liabilities	Balance
Real Estate	$400,000	Mortgage	$184,685
Checking/Savings	$50,000	Credit Cards	$0
Retirement Accounts	$0	Auto Loans	$0
Total Assets	$450,000	Total Liabilities	$184,685
		Net Worth	$265,315

Figure 2. Mrs. Miller's balance sheet and net worth.

Fortunately for Mrs. Miller, her home has appreciated nicely in recent years and is now worth $400,000. However, she has no plans to sell. She loves her home and wants to live in it for the rest of her life.

With $50,000 in the bank and over $215,000 worth of home equity, Mrs. Miller has a substantial net worth, but only $50,000 of it (her savings) is *liquid*. The rest of her net worth is locked away in *non* liquid home equity.

With only $50,000 in liquid assets and a negative cash flow of nearly $1,100 per month, Mrs. Miller will run out of money in about four years. If she gets hit with a big unexpected expense such as a home repair or medical bill, her savings will be wiped out even sooner.

Let's make a few observations before we proceed from here. With a mortgage payment of just over $1,100 and a negative cash flow of around $1,100, Mrs. Miller is essentially draining her liquid cash reserves to pay her mortgage. She has twenty-three years to go before the mortgage is paid off, so it's a good bet the mortgage will outlive her. It makes no sense for Mrs. Miller to drain her savings for a mortgage she may not live long enough to pay off anyway. She's throwing good money after bad!

Because Mrs. Miller doesn't have a lot of income, refinancing is out of the question. She simply doesn't qualify. Even if she *could* qualify, there's no way she can reduce the mortgage payment enough to solve her negative cash flow problem.

It also doesn't make sense to take out a home equity line of credit, or HELOC. She won't qualify because of her income. And even if she could, how does it help to add yet another monthly expense to an already impossible budget? Mrs. Miller doesn't need to *increase* her expenses, she needs to get her expenses *down*!

Fortunately, this is where the reverse mortgage comes in. It's the perfect solution! A reverse mortgage would enable Mrs. Miller to get rid of her mortgage payment and stay in her home while solving her cash flow problem and protecting her remaining savings.

Based on her age and a home value of $400,000, Mrs. Miller qualifies for a reverse mortgage principal limit of $199,600. Remember, the principal limit is the total gross amount available from the reverse mortgage before paying off mandatory obligations like existing mortgages, closing costs, set asides, etc.

Mrs. Miller chooses the variable-rate HECM because it offers more money than the fixed-rate HECM. The initial interest rate for the variable-rate HECM is 4.52%, which is lower than the rate for the fixed-rate HECM. When the MIP of 0.50% is added in, the total interest rate is 5.02%.

Because Mrs. Miller has a fairly large starting loan balance, she is able to negotiate a $9,000 lender credit to cover part of her closing costs. Remember, a lender credit is essentially a payment from the lender for purposes of covering closing costs.

As you can see in Figure 3, after paying off her mortgage balance and net closing costs, Mrs. Miller is left with $9,915 from the principal limit that can be used to supplement her savings. She decides to take the entire $9,915 at closing, so the starting reverse mortgage balance equals the $199,600 principal limit amount.

Case Studies

Reverse Mortgage Summary

Payoffs and Costs		Interest Rates	
Principal Limit (PL)	$199,600	Initial Interest Rate (IIR)	4.52%
Mortgage Payoff	-$184,685	Annual MIP	0.50%
IMIP	-$8,000	**Total Interest Rate**	**5.02%**
Origination	-$3,200		
3rd Party Costs	-$2,800		
Lender Credit	$9,000		
Net Principal Limit	**$9,915**		

Figure 3. A breakdown of Mrs. Miller's reverse mortgage, including principal limit, mortgage payoff, closing costs, and interest rates.

Mrs. Miller considered leaving the money in a line of credit because of the growth rate, but she felt better having the cash in her savings account. Her savings account balance has been a source of peace of mind since her husband died. As far as she's concerned, the higher the balance, the better she feels about it.

Now let's look at how the reverse mortgage balance changes over time. Assuming Mrs. Miller doesn't make any mortgage payments (the whole point, right?), interest and MIP will accrue onto the loan balance over time. The numbers are broken down in Figure 4.

Reverse Mortgage Amortization

Year	Age	MIP	IIR	Loan Balance	Payment Savings
0	75	0.50%	4.52%	$199,600	$13,527
1	76	0.50%	4.52%	$209,854	$13,527
2	77	0.50%	4.52%	$220,634	$13,527
3	78	0.50%	4.52%	$231,968	$13,527
4	79	0.50%	4.52%	$243,885	$13,527
5	80	0.50%	4.52%	$256,414	$13,527
6	81	0.50%	4.52%	$269,586	$13,527
7	82	0.50%	4.52%	$283,435	$13,527
8	83	0.50%	4.52%	$297,995	$13,527
9	84	0.50%	4.52%	$313,304	$13,527
10	85	0.50%	4.52%	$329,399	$13,527
11	86	0.50%	4.52%	$346,320	$13,527
12	87	0.50%	4.52%	$364,111	$13,527
13	88	0.50%	4.52%	$382,816	$13,527
14	89	0.50%	4.52%	$402,482	$13,527
15	90	0.50%	4.52%	$423,158	$13,527
16	91	0.50%	4.52%	$444,896	$13,527
17	92	0.50%	4.52%	$467,751	$13,527
18	93	0.50%	4.52%	$491,780	$13,527
19	94	0.50%	4.52%	$517,043	$13,527
20	95	0.50%	4.52%	$543,604	$13,527

Figure 4. How Mrs. Miller's reverse mortgage amortizes over time.

As you can see, if Mrs. Miller lives another 20 years, her balance will grow to over $543,000. Yes, this is a substantial increase! However, let's not forget the other side of the equation: over that same 20-year period, Mrs. Miller will have saved over $270,000 that otherwise would have gone to mortgage payments. That's $270,000 that enabled her to protect and preserve her lifestyle, peace of mind, and savings.

Let's also not forget that Mrs. Miller isn't leaving a big mess for her heirs to clean up. The HECM is a non recourse loan, which means the most that's ever paid back is the value of the home. If the loan balance ever exceeds the value of her home, FHA's insurance fund will cover the shortage.

Once the reverse mortgage is complete and the mortgage payment is gone, Mrs. Miller will have a positive cash flow of $45 per month. Granted, she's not going to be taking world cruises or buying expensive cars on that kind of money. She still doesn't have a ton of wiggle room in the monthly budget. However, the reverse mortgage substantially improved her monthly cash flow situation. As far as Mrs. Miller is concerned, it's more than good enough to no longer worry about running out of money or having to sell her home because of a big mortgage payment.

The reverse mortgage also sparked some productive conversations with her adult children. She never liked to talk to her kids about money, but she felt she needed to let them know about the reverse mortgage and why she chose to get one. Now that they know more about her financial situation, they've volunteered to kick in some additional money every month to help her out.

Mrs. Miller even decided to take a part-time job for a few hours per week. Yes, she has some health issues, but the reverse mortgage already got rid of the mortgage payment. She no longer feels the financial pressure to work a lot of hours to cover her mortgage payment. She figures she'll work a few hours every week to get out of the house, make some new friends, and make a few extra bucks.

Case study #2: Converting home equity into a tax-free and growing retirement "account"

Mr. and Mrs. Nelson, both 64, are retired and living in Texas. Mr. Nelson was an insurance agent and Mrs. Nelson worked for a small accounting firm. They made decent money, stayed out of debt, saved diligently, and managed to retire with a paid off house and a combined $300,000 in their traditional IRAs.

Though the Nelsons have substantial retirement assets and no debt, they still live on a tight budget. Their combined Social Security income of $3,000 per month covers their living expenses, but it doesn't leave much for emergencies or fun activities. Check out Figure 1 below, which summarizes the Nelsons' monthly cash flow.

Case Studies

Income and Expenses

Income	Expenses	Cash Flow
$3,000	-$2,855	$145

Figure 1. The Nelsons' monthly income, expenses, and cash flow.

As you can see, they have just $145 left over at the end of the month, which isn't enough to pay for unexpected expenses like car repairs, home repairs, or medical bills. It's also not enough to pay for travel and other fun activities. Yes, they could tap into their IRAs for additional income, but they're still relatively young and want to leave their IRAs untouched for as long as possible.

The Nelsons are concerned about the future impact of inflation. If their budget is tight now, what will it be like in ten years when the cost of everything has gone up? Yes, they'll get occasional raises from Social Security, but those aren't nearly enough to keep up with real-world inflation. The Nelsons need an additional source of income so they can have more fun and worry less about unexpected expenses.

Before we go further, let's check out the Nelsons' balance sheet, which is summarized in Figure 2. As you can see, they have no debt and have accumulated a nice nest egg in their IRAs. On top of that, their home has appreciated considerably over the years to a current value of $250,000.

Case Studies

Balance Sheet and Net Worth

Assets	Asset Value	Liabilities	Balance
Real Estate	$250,000	Mortgage	$0
Checking/Savings	$3,000	Credit Cards	$0
Retirement Accounts	$300,000	Auto Loans	$0
Total Assets	$553,000	Total Liabilities	$0
		Net Worth	$553,000

Figure 2. The Nelsons' balance sheet and net worth.

Though the Nelsons have a net worth of over half a million dollars, 45% of it is in the form of home equity. Now, home equity is great to have, but it's not liquid. You can't exchange your home equity for plane tickets to Hawaii, a new roof, or critical medical care, right?

The other 55% of the Nelsons' net worth is in their IRAs. Though the IRAs are accessible and liquid, withdrawals come with the pitfall of income taxes. On top of that, the Nelsons recognize that people are living much longer these days. It's possible they could live another 20 to 25 years, so they want to make sure their money lasts. They don't want to touch their IRAs until they're forced to start taking required minimum distributions.

Now, there *are* a few traditional ways the Nelsons could convert home equity into cash. They could get a cash out mortgage or home equity line of credit (HELOC), but that means taking on a mortgage payment for the next 20 to 30 years. Their budget is already tight, so the last thing they need is another payment. They're also aware of how a HELOC recast works and don't want that headache in the future when they're older and in potentially declining health.

The other option is to downsize. They could sell their home and buy a smaller and cheaper home for cash and put the difference in the bank to live on. But with realtor fees, closing costs, and moving expenses figured in, they doubt they can make it work without seriously compromising their lifestyle. Besides, they like their home and neighborhood. They have good friends on their street and their children and grandchildren live nearby.

They could take part-time jobs to make extra fun money, but they have zero desire to do that. They'd rather spend the time traveling and enjoying their grandchildren.

The Nelsons need an additional income source that allows them to stay in their home, avoid touching their IRAs, and avoid taking part-time jobs. Fortunately, a HECM is the perfect solution! In fact, the Nelsons are ideal candidates for a HECM because they owe nothing on their home and don't need all the proceeds right now. They can leave the vast majority of the proceeds in a growing line of credit that can be tapped in the future for splurges or unexpected expenses.

Based on their ages and home value, the Nelsons qualify for an adjustable-rate HECM with an initial line of credit of $97,200 after closing costs. Figure 3 summarizes the numbers.

Case Studies

Reverse Mortgage Summary

Payoffs and Costs		Interest Rates	
Principal Limit (PL)	$107,500	Initial Interest Rate (IIR)	4.52%
Mortgage Payoff	$0	Annual MIP	0.50%
IMIP	-$5,000	**Total Interest Rate**	**5.02%**
Origination	-$2,500		
3rd Party Costs	-$2,800		
Lender Credit	$0		
Net Principal Limit	**$97,200**		

Figure 3. A breakdown of the Nelsons' reverse mortgage, including principal limit, mortgage payoff, closing costs, and interest rates.

The initial interest rate is 4.52%, which means the total interest rate is 5.02% after adding the MIP. The growth rate on the line of credit always equals the total interest rate, so it is 5.02% as well. If the initial interest rate increases in the future, the growth rate will increase as well, which means the line of credit will grow and compound *faster*.

The Nelson's love that the line of credit will always grow as long as at least one of them is living in the home and paying the required property charges. They can see how the HECM line of credit isn't like a HELOC, which can be chopped, frozen, or taken away on a whim by the lender. The HECM line of credit will always be available as long as they fulfill their program obligations.

It's even possible for the line of credit to grow larger than the value of the home. If that happens, the Nelsons have beat the system, so to speak. The HECM is a non recourse loan, so they could withdraw every last penny but not be on the hook for any more than their home is worth. This protects their equity for their use against the whims of an often volatile real estate market.

The Nelsons don't need any money right now, so they choose not to take any cash at closing. All of the available proceeds will be allocated to the line of credit, which they can tap at will in the future. This means the starting loan balance is $10,300 because of the closing costs.

Figure 4 shows how the reverse mortgage balance and line of credit change over time. Note that these projections assume the initial interest rate doesn't change and the Nelsons don't take any cash from the reverse mortgage. Obviously, that's not realistic, but it's all we have to go on at the moment. If rates increase, the line of credit will grow faster. If the Nelsons withdraw funds from the line of credit, the remaining available line of credit will be smaller, but it will still grow.

Reverse Mortgage Amortization

Year	Age	MIP	IIR	Loan Balance	Line of Credit
0	64	0.50%	4.52%	$10,300	$97,200
1	65	0.50%	4.52%	$10,829	$102,193
2	66	0.50%	4.52%	$11,385	$107,443
3	67	0.50%	4.52%	$11,970	$112,963
4	68	0.50%	4.52%	$12,585	$118,766
5	69	0.50%	4.52%	$13,232	$124,867
6	70	0.50%	4.52%	$13,911	$131,281
7	71	0.50%	4.52%	$14,626	$138,025
8	72	0.50%	4.52%	$15,378	$145,116
9	73	0.50%	4.52%	$16,167	$152,571
10	74	0.50%	4.52%	$16,998	$160,408
11	75	0.50%	4.52%	$17,871	$168,649
12	76	0.50%	4.52%	$18,789	$177,313
13	77	0.50%	4.52%	$19,755	$186,421
14	78	0.50%	4.52%	$20,769	$195,998
15	79	0.50%	4.52%	$21,836	$206,067
16	80	0.50%	4.52%	$22,958	$216,653
17	81	0.50%	4.52%	$24,137	$227,782
18	82	0.50%	4.52%	$25,377	$239,484
19	83	0.50%	4.52%	$26,681	$251,786
20	84	0.50%	4.52%	$28,052	$264,721
21	85	0.50%	4.52%	$29,493	$278,320
22	86	0.50%	4.52%	$31,008	$292,618
23	87	0.50%	4.52%	$32,601	$307,650
24	88	0.50%	4.52%	$34,276	$323,454
25	89	0.50%	4.52%	$36,036	$340,071
26	90	0.50%	4.52%	$37,888	$357,540

Figure 4. How the Nelsons' reverse mortgage balance and line of credit amortizes over time.

As you can see, the line of credit can grow to a very large amount indeed. If left untouched, it will grow to well over a quarter of a million dollars in just twenty years. That's money the Nelsons can tap whenever they like, *tax free*, with just a phone call to their lender.

Now, let's make a few observations about what the Nelsons have gained by getting a HECM line of credit. First of all, they now have more fun money available without adding a mortgage payment, working part-time, downsizing, or draining their IRAs (and incurring a tax bill in the process).

They've also gained an additional emergency reserve that can be tapped to pay for unexpected expenses. They no longer need to worry about draining their IRAs to pay for medical bills or home repairs.

The reverse mortgage has also enabled the Nelsons to convert a largely unusable resource—home equity—into a liquid and performing retirement "account". No longer will they need to rely solely on their taxable IRAs for liquidity. The HECM line of credit has increased their liquid assets by over 30%, which helps protect and preserve their lifestyle and other retirement assets for longer.

The Nelsons are hugely excited about the possibilities offered by their new reverse mortgage. They can have more fun, worry less, and protect the longevity of their assets in the process.

Case study #3: Converting home equity into a tax-free income stream

Mrs. Harris is a 75-year-old widow living in beautiful southern Utah. She's been retired for 8 years and lives on a modest income consisting of Social Security and a small pension totaling $1,807 per month. Her income was adequate for her needs when she retired, but her expenses have risen due to inflation and she now finds herself struggling to cover even the basics.

As you can see in Figure 1, Mrs. Harris' basic living expenses add up to $1,735, which leaves her a mere $72 at the end of the month. Because she's running so tight, Mrs. Harris has cut back on her favorite activities—bowling and golf—to make ends meet.

Income and Expenses

Income	Expenses	Cash Flow
$1,807	-$1,735	$72

Figure 1. Mrs. Harris' monthly income, expenses, and cash flow.

Mrs. Harris is worried about getting hit with a big unexpected expense, such as a medical bill or home repair. Her car is getting a little long in the tooth, too. It's a good bet she'll need to pay for significant car repairs and maintenance in the near future.

In the past, Mrs. Harris maintained a large emergency savings account to pay for unexpected expenses, which kept her out of credit card debt. But now she has to tap into her savings on a regular basis just to cover her living expenses. Her savings account, which used to be over $30,000, has dwindled to a mere $1,200. She's well aware that a few home or car repairs can wipe out what's left in no time.

Mrs. Harris is tired of stressing about money, so she decides to inquire about a reverse mortgage. A HECM is the perfect solution because it allows her to convert a large portion of her home's equity into an income stream that will help protect her lifestyle and financial security. Fortunately, Mrs. Harris (and her late husband) paid off their house years before retirement and it has appreciated considerably since then. Because she has no mortgage, she has the maximum equity available to convert to income.

Figure 2 summarizes Mrs. Harris' balance sheet. As you can see, she has a nice net worth on paper, but a mere $1,200 of it is liquid. The other $350,000 is locked away in her home's equity and can't be used for anything.

Balance Sheet and Net Worth

Assets	Asset Value	Liabilities	Balance
Real Estate	$350,000	Mortgage	$0
Checking/Savings	$1,200	Credit Cards	$0
Retirement Accounts	$0	Auto Loans	$0
Total Assets	**$351,200**	**Total Liabilities**	**$0**
		Net Worth	$351,200

Figure 2. Mrs. Harris' balance sheet and net worth.

Home equity is great to have, but unfortunately, it's not very useful unless it can be converted into cash. Fortunately for Mrs. Harris, that's exactly where the reverse mortgage comes in. Based on her age and home value, Mrs. Harris qualifies for a principal limit of $192,850. Remember, the principal limit is the gross amount available before paying off closing costs, existing mortgage balances, set asides, etc.

The closing costs (IMIP, origination, and 3rd-party costs) total $13,300 and are rolled into the starting loan balance. This leaves Mrs. Harris with a net principal limit of $179,550 that can be allocated to a lump sum, term/tenure income, line of credit, or some combination of all of these options. Figure 3 shows a break down of the numbers.

Reverse Mortgage Summary

Payoffs and Costs		Interest Rates	
Principal Limit (PL)	$192,850	Initial Interest Rate (IIR)	4.52%
Mortgage Payoff	$0	Annual MIP	0.50%
IMIP	-$7,000	**Total Interest Rate**	**5.02%**
Origination	-$3,500		
3rd Party Costs	-$2,800		
Lender Credit	$0		
Net Principal Limit	**$179,550**		

Figure 3. A breakdown of Mrs. Harris' reverse mortgage, including principal limit, mortgage payoff, closing costs, and interest rates.

Mrs. Harris opts for a tenure plan, which offers a guaranteed lifetime income of $1,203.86 per month. She'll receive this income for the rest of her life regardless of how long she lives or if she uses up all the equity in her home. As long as she lives in and maintains the home and pays her required property charges (property taxes, homeowner's insurance, special assessments, etc.), she'll receive her tenure payments. And if she ultimately borrows more than the home is worth, she won't leave a mess for her heirs to clean up because the HECM is a non recourse loan. FHA's mortgage insurance fund will cover any shortage.

Mrs. Harris tries to negotiate a lender credit to cover some of her closing costs, but the lender is unable to accommodate. Her starting loan balance is just too small. As her originator explains, the starting balance doesn't generate enough interest for the lender to absorb the closing costs without taking a big loss on the loan. Obviously, the lender can't stay in business by losing money.

Figure 4 shows how the loan balance will increase over time as Mrs. Harris draws her tenure payments. If the home appreciates at the historical national average of 4%, which is assumed in the numbers, she will have substantial equity in her home for the rest of her life. Even if she uses up every last penny of equity, she'll still receive her tenure payment month in and month out.

Reverse Mortgage Amortization

Year	Age	MIP	IIR	Loan Balance	Home Value	Equity
0	75	0.50%	4.52%	$13,300	$350,000	$336,700
1	76	0.50%	4.52%	$28,828	$364,000	$335,172
2	77	0.50%	4.52%	$45,155	$378,560	$333,405
3	78	0.50%	4.52%	$62,320	$393,702	$331,383
4	79	0.50%	4.52%	$80,366	$409,450	$329,084
5	80	0.50%	4.52%	$99,340	$425,829	$326,489
6	81	0.50%	4.52%	$119,288	$442,862	$323,573
7	82	0.50%	4.52%	$140,262	$460,576	$320,315
8	83	0.50%	4.52%	$162,312	$478,999	$316,687
9	84	0.50%	4.52%	$185,496	$498,159	$312,663
10	85	0.50%	4.52%	$209,870	$518,085	$308,215
11	86	0.50%	4.52%	$235,497	$538,809	$303,312
12	87	0.50%	4.52%	$262,440	$560,361	$297,922
13	88	0.50%	4.52%	$290,767	$582,776	$292,009
14	89	0.50%	4.52%	$320,549	$606,087	$285,538
15	90	0.50%	4.52%	$351,861	$630,330	$278,469
16	91	0.50%	4.52%	$384,782	$655,543	$270,761
17	92	0.50%	4.52%	$419,394	$681,765	$262,371
18	93	0.50%	4.52%	$455,784	$709,036	$253,252
19	94	0.50%	4.52%	$494,043	$737,397	$243,354
20	95	0.50%	4.52%	$534,268	$766,893	$232,625
21	96	0.50%	4.52%	$576,560	$797,569	$221,009
22	97	0.50%	4.52%	$621,023	$829,472	$208,448
23	98	0.50%	4.52%	$667,771	$862,650	$194,879
24	99	0.50%	4.52%	$716,921	$897,156	$180,236

Figure 4. How Mrs. Harris' reverse mortgage balance amortizes over time. Even though she's drawing on her equity every month, she'll likely have substantial equity in her home for the rest of her life if her home appreciates at the historical national average of 4%.

Mrs. Harris is extremely excited about the reverse mortgage. Getting another $1,200 per month in income is literally *life changing* for her. She plans to start bowling and golfing again, getting some repairs done on her car, and building up her emergency savings. She might even gather up some friends and go on a cruise she's been eyeballing for years but couldn't afford. But most importantly, Mrs. Harris can once again rest easy at night and no longer worry about money.

Case study #4: How a HECM can protect and preserve your retirement assets for longer

One of the most devastating financial risks in retirement is one you've possibly never heard of. Unfortunately, many seniors fall prey to this danger completely unaware of it and run out of money years faster than they expect. What is this danger? It's called *sequence risk*, or *sequence of returns* risk. My goal with this case study is to show how a reverse mortgage can significantly reduce sequence risk and help preserve your retirement assets for longer.

Most people save for retirement during their working years by buying stocks, mutual funds, ETFs, etc., through a 401(k) or IRA. They build up a retirement nest egg by accumulating shares that (hopefully) increase in value and/or generate a return over time.

When you retire, you do the opposite. You're no longer working, so you *sell* shares in your retirement account and use the proceeds as income. The challenge is striking the right balance between generating income and preserving your assets so they last at least as long as you do. If you drain your assets too fast, you risk running out of money before you die. If you don't withdraw enough, you'll preserve your assets for longer, but risk missing out on the retirement lifestyle you worked decades to earn.

Financial professionals and pundits like to point out that the S&P 500 stock index has achieved a 10% average return since its inception in 1928. That's a great statistic, but it's misleading. After all, the stock market doesn't go up in a steady and straight line. If it did, saving for retirement would be pretty easy, right? The stock market goes up and down and *over the long term* it returns the average 10% we all hear about.

What kind of market will it be when you retire? Will you get lucky and retire at the start of a long bull market? What if you retire at the start of a devastating bear market? What if the value of the shares in your retirement account drops by half just as you quit your job? If your shares drop by half, you now need to sell *twice* the number of shares to achieve the same income target. You're now draining your retirement assets *faster*, which means you're at risk of running out of money sooner.

This is the essence of sequence risk. It's the risk you'll encounter a bear market early in retirement, causing you to drain your retirement assets faster than expected. Sequence risk is that lurking predator waiting to devour the assets you worked hard to build during your working years. It's almost impossible to see it coming because it's impossible to predict exactly when the next bear market will begin.

When you're retired, you don't have the capacity to earn like you did in decades past. If you want a financially secure retirement and want to defend against sequence risk, it's essential to have as many financial options as possible. To show how a reverse mortgage can reduce sequence risk and protect your nest egg for longer, let's look at a few scenarios based on real-world data. Note that we'll disregard income taxes for the sake of simplicity.

Scenario #1: How sequence risk destroys retirement assets

Let's assume it's January 2007 and Andrew, a former accountant, has just retired with a free and clear house and a 401(k) worth $191,900. To protect his nest egg, Andrew plans to move his entire 401(k) into ABALX, a conservative balanced mutual fund (note this isn't intended as investment advice). Balanced funds are often a good choice for retirees because they're diversified over a variety of assets to provide safer and more conservative returns.

Andrew recently started taking Social Security, but it isn't enough to cover his expenses. He plans to withdraw $1,000 from his 401(k) every month to make up for the income shortfall.

Andrew moves his 401(k) into ABALX at the end of September 2007 and purchases exactly 10,000 shares at $19.19/share. He takes his first $1,000 withdrawal at the beginning of October 2007.

Well, we all know what happens next. The stock market declines badly all through 2008 and finally bottoms in early 2009. Unfortunately, as the share price of ABALX falls, Andrew is forced to sell more shares to achieve the same $1,000 income he needs to cover his expenses.

Back in October 2007, he only needed 53 shares to yield $1,000 ($1,017.07 to be exact). At the market bottom in February 2009, it takes 84 shares to get $1,000. Yikes! He's draining his assets much faster than planned and he's starting to worry. He's just two years into retirement and he's already sold over 1,500 of his original 10,000 shares of ABALX.

Andrew is confident the market will recover, but when? He's burning through shares so fast he'll have hardly any left to rebuild his account balance once the market recovers. The market will recover at some point, but will his account last until then? Andrew needs the income, so he hopes for the best and continues taking his $1,000 every month.

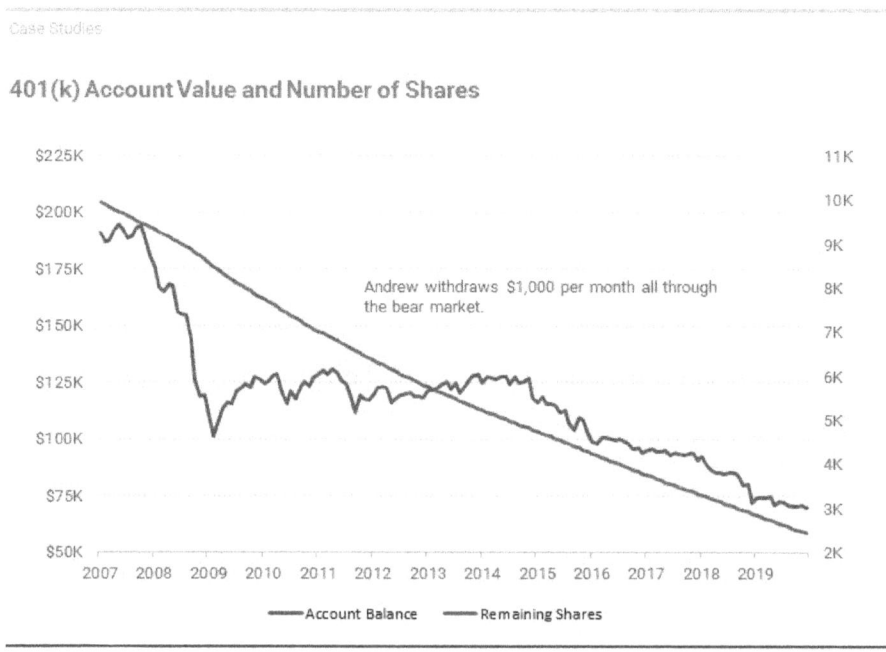

Figure 1. *Andrew withdraws $1,000 per month from his 401(k) all through the bear market.*

Now, let's fast forward to December 2019. How is Andrew's 401(k) holding up? Unfortunately, not well. Figure 1 shows the damage done to his account balance. The 10-year bull market since 2009 has increased the value of his remaining shares, but his account balance is now just under $75,000. Andrew has only 2,447 of his original 10,000 shares left. He's blown through over 3/4 of his shares in twelve years. Not good! Andrew is in danger of running out of money much earlier than anticipated.

Unfortunately, Andrew's 401(k) and future financial security have fallen prey to sequence risk. He needed the income to cover his expenses, so he had no choice but to be a seller during the bear market years. He's drained his 401(k) and is facing the very real prospect of outliving his money.

Now, what if Andrew had another asset to rely on in addition to his 401(k)? What if he had a reverse mortgage line of credit that could have been tapped so he didn't need to sell shares in a declining market? As we'll see, he not only would have had far more liquid assets to live on, but he would have preserved his 401(k) much better.

Scenario #2: How a reverse mortgage can protect and preserve retirement assets

Let's take a time machine back to January 2007 and once again assume Andrew has just retired. This time, however, let's assume we're in an alternate universe and he's heard about how a HECM line of credit grows and compounds over time. He figures he has tons of home equity just sitting there doing nothing, so he wants to put it to work. It's a good idea to have as many financial options as possible, right? After all, you never know when the next bear market might hit, right?

Let's assume that Andrew's HECM line of credit starts off at $100,600 and his annual growth rate is 5.96%. Andrew's plan is to leave the line of credit untouched and let it grow until he needs it.

Let's again assume Andrew moves his 401(k) into 10,000 shares of ABALX in September 2007 and sets up a $1,000/month withdrawal that will start in October 2007. Just a few days before his first check is sent in October 2007,

Andrew gets nervous about the markets. He's seen all the headlines about bad subprime mortgages and is worried about what impact it will have on his 401(k). He decides to cancel the withdrawal from the 401(k) and start taking $1,000/month from his HECM line of credit instead. By this time, he's already enjoyed 10 months of growth and his line of credit is now worth $105,187.

Well, we all know what happened in the stock market in 2008 and 2009. It's painful to watch his 401(k) decline in value, but Andrew holds firm with the belief that it will recover at some point. In the meantime, at least his income is secure and he's not selling shares into a declining market.

Andrew leaves his 401(k) completely untouched while the market declines. In fact, he leaves the 401(k) untouched for a full five years until it once again recovers back to the same value it was in September 2007.

In September 2012, Andrew decides to stop his withdrawals from the line of credit and instead start taking money from the 401(k). His first $1,000 payment from the 401(k) arrives in October 2012. His 401(k) is now worth $200,393 and the available HECM line of credit is worth $71,911. Andrew has a total of $272,304 in liquid assets available. Not bad, right?

Let's fast forward to December 2019 and see how things look. Andrew has left his HECM line of credit alone for the last seven years to let it grow and has continued to draw $1,000 per month from his 401(k). Check out the results in Figure 2.

As of December 2019, the 401(k) is worth $184,993—just a little less than where it started over a decade ago. Yes, the balance took a big hit through the bad bear market in 2008 and 2009. However, Andrew was able to recoup all of his losses because he had an alternate source of income (the HECM) and didn't have to sell shares during the bear market years. He preserved more than $100,000 worth of account value versus Andrew in Scenario #1. Even better, the HECM line of credit still has $110,112 available. That too, is roughly the same amount as when he retired nearly 12 years ago.

401(k) Account Value and Number of Shares

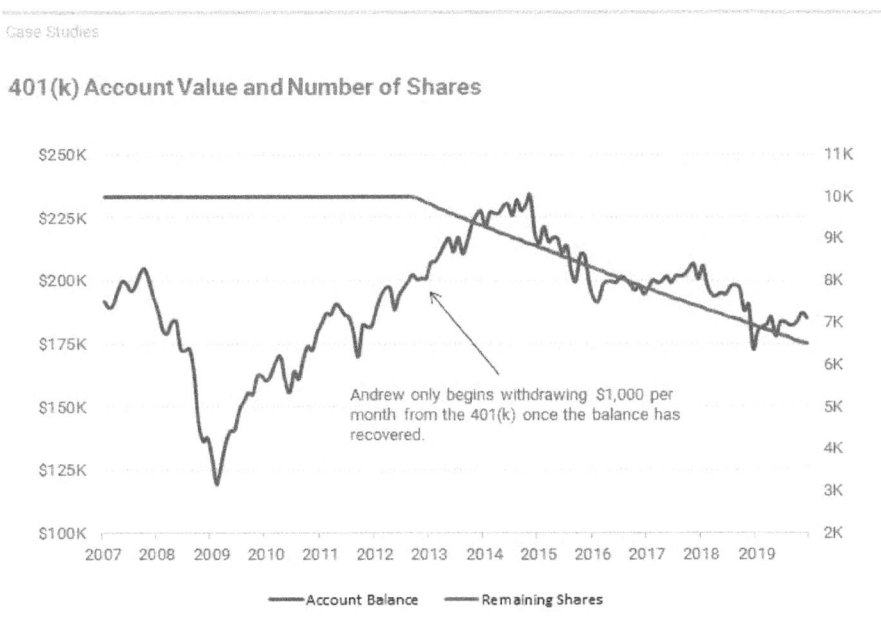

Figure 2. Because Andrew was able to live on his HECM line of credit, he was able to better protect and preserve his 401(k).

By having more than one financial option, Andrew was able to pick and choose what asset to tap into based on market conditions. He was able to protect his assets and lifestyle much more effectively from one of the worst bear markets in memory.

As you can see in the Figure 3, below, the results speak for themselves. The Andrew in Scenario #1 (the bottom line in red) has already burned through well over half of his liquid retirement assets by the end of 2019. This is especially worrisome because another bear market will likely wipe him out completely.

Total Liquid Assets With and Without the HECM LOC

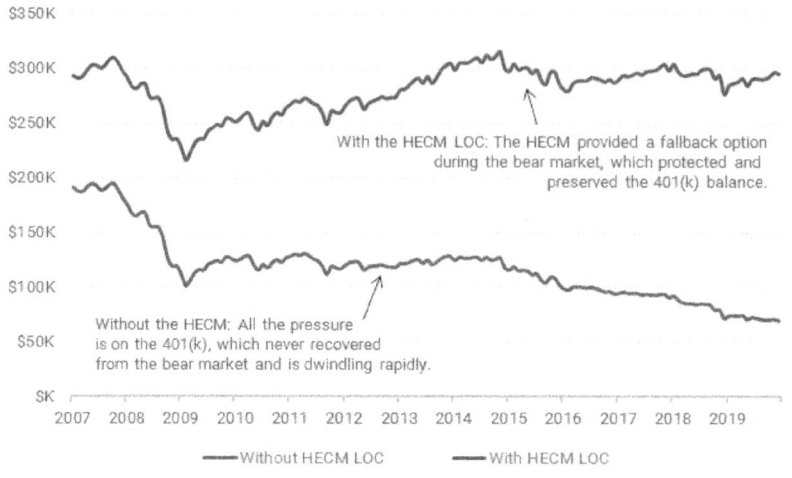

Figure 3. It's pretty clear that the HECM line of credit helped Andrew in Scenario #2 better protect his liquid assets and financial security.

On the other hand, the Andrew in Scenario #2 (the top line in blue) has done *far* better. Because he had more than one financial option, he was able to pick and choose what asset to tap into based on market conditions. He was not only able to preserve his assets, but he has over $200,000 *more* liquid assets to live on than the Andrew in Scenario #1.

Folks, it's pretty clear: 401(k) plus HECM line of credit is the winner against the sequence risk monster. The HECM line of credit can help preserve your retirement assets and lifestyle for much longer.

As we've seen in this case study, there is tremendous financial security in having multiple financial options. If you have more than one income source in retirement, you can more effectively protect and preserve your assets and lifestyle against changes in the turbulent financial markets. You can pick and choose what income source to tap into based on market conditions. If your retirement account has taken a beating in a down market, you can leave it alone and tap into the HECM until the market recovers. After the market recovers, you can once again tap into your retirement account and leave the HECM line of credit alone to grow and compound.

Case study #5: How one woman purchased a "forever home" she couldn't otherwise afford

Anna, aged 67, is a retired teacher who lives in Virginia. Anna loves Virginia, but she wants to move closer to her sister Donna, who recently moved to the Seattle area. Anna and Donna have always been close and Anna is like a second mother to Donna's two teenage girls.

Anna is excited about moving to Seattle, but she's worried about affording a home there. She's paid down much of her mortgage balance and her home has appreciated considerably over the years, but Donna lives in a more expensive area. Anna is concerned that she can't afford a home near her sister.

Before we proceed further, let's check out Anna's current cash flow situation. As you can see in Figure 1, Anna has a good income. She receives a combined $4,031 from her teacher's pension and her late husband's Social Security.

Case Studies

Income and Expenses

Income	Expenses	Cash Flow
$4,031	-$3,752	$279

Figure 1. Anna's monthly income, expenses, and cash flow.

However, she also has high expenses, mainly because of her mortgage payment. Her total monthly expenses are $3,752, which includes a mortgage principal and interest payment of $1,104.51. This leaves her with just $279 left over at the end of the month. She's not broke, but that's not a lot of money to do fun things with.

Let's also check out Anna's balance sheet, which is shown in Figure 2. As you can see, Anna has $10,000 in checking and savings and a modest balance of $97,000 in her retirement account. The retirement account balance isn't large enough to live on, but she's not worried about it because she has a decent pension. She considers the retirement account to be emergency money that can be tapped for unexpected expenses.

Case Studies

Balance Sheet and Net Worth

Assets	Asset Value	Liabilities	Balance
Real Estate	$450,000	Mortgage	$132,251
Checking/Savings	$10,000	Credit Cards	$2,000
Retirement Accounts	$97,000	Auto Loans	$0
Total Assets	**$557,000**	**Total Liabilities**	**$134,251**
		Net Worth	$422,749

Figure 2. Anna's assets, liabilities, and net worth.

Anna's only liabilities are her mortgage and a credit card balance of $2,000. She paid off her car a few years ago and has no plans to replace it any time soon.

Anna's home has appreciated nicely over the years and is currently worth around $450,000, but her mortgage balance is over $132,000 and won't be paid off for another 15 years. She has over $300,000 in equity, but it's not enough to purchase a home for cash near her sister. She really wants to buy for cash so she's not stuck with a mortgage payment for the rest of her life. She's on a tight budget now and doesn't want to live that way in Seattle.

Once you figure in realtor fees, moving costs, and closing costs (for both the sale and the new purchase), Anna will probably net around $280,000 from the sale of her home. Unfortunately, the typical home near her sister costs around $500,000. Anna just doesn't have enough to work with to buy a home for cash and avoid a big mortgage payment.

Fortunately, Anna has a close friend who is an experienced and savvy realtor. Her friend is one of the relatively few realtors out there who are familiar with the HECM for purchase program. To her surprise, Anna learns that she can finance the purchase of a home *without* a mortgage payment using a HECM reverse mortgage. Anna calls a lender her realtor friend knows and discovers that, yes, she *can* buy a home near her sister without paying all cash to avoid a mortgage payment.

Anna flies out to Seattle and quickly gets a great home under contract for $490,000. Based on the purchase price and her age, Anna qualifies for a principal limit of $275,380. In other words, the lender will finance $275,380 with no mortgage payment as long as Anna lives in the home and pays the required property charges. The difference between the purchase price and the principal limit, which is $214,620, is Anna's down payment. Anna will need to pay the closing costs out of pocket in addition to the down payment.

Case Studies

Reverse Mortgage Summary

Payoffs and Costs		Interest Rates	
Principal Limit (PL)	$275,380	Initial Interest Rate (IIR)	4.52%
Purchase Price	-$490,000	Annual MIP	0.50%
IMIP	-$9,800	**Total Interest Rate**	**5.02%**
Origination	-$4,900		
3rd Party Costs	-$3,063		
Lender Credit	$10,000		
Cash to Close	**-$222,383**		

Figure 3. A breakdown of Anna's reverse mortgage. She'll need just $222,383 to close the purchase of her new home.

Fortunately, because interest rate conditions are favorable and she's starting with a decent-sized loan balance, Anna is able to negotiate a $10,000 lender credit. This means her net closing costs total $7,763. As shown in Figure 3, her total cash to close, including down payment and closing costs, is $222,383. That means she'll have over $50,000 left over after the down payment and closing costs from the $280,000 she'll have after selling her Virginia home.

Not too shabby!

Let's make a few observations about what just happened here. First of all, Anna was able to purchase a home *without a mortgage payment* that she otherwise couldn't afford to buy outright. Yes, Anna could have put $280,000 down and financed the rest with a traditional 30-year fixed mortgage. Rates are lower now than when she bought her home in Virginia, so she likely could qualify for and afford such a loan. However, it would have meant being stuck with a big mortgage payment for the next 30 years. Anna is concerned about unexpected expenses in the future, like home repairs and medical bills. She also wants to have extra money to travel and spoil her nieces. For Anna, it just wasn't an option to buy a house in Seattle with another big mortgage payment. Financially, it would make more sense to just stay in Virginia and pay off the mortgage she already had in the next 15 years.

Anna couldn't afford to buy her new home with *cash* to avoid a mortgage payment, but she was still able to avoid a mortgage payment. The HECM significantly increased her purchasing power and enabled her to *finance* part of the purchase without a mortgage payment. Without the HECM, Anna would only be able to purchase a home outright that was priced up to $270,000 or $280,000 because that was all the cash she had to work with. The HECM enabled her to purchase a $490,000 home – *and still avoid a mortgage payment.* The HECM *significantly* increased her purchasing power.

Let's also not forget that Anna was able to shed her old mortgage payment, which increased her disposable income by around $1,100 per month. This significantly enhances her financial freedom and lifestyle. She now has extra money to do the fun things she couldn't afford in Virginia. She also wiped out her credit card balance, which further improved her monthly cash flow.

Even better, Anna was able to significantly boost her retirement nest egg. She walked away from the sale of her Virginia home with $280,000, but only needed $222,383 to close the sale on a more expensive home in Seattle. After paying off her $2,000 credit card balance, she was able to add $55,617 to her savings account and improve her long-term financial security.

In short, the HECM reverse mortgage enabled Anna to move close to her sister, purchase a home she couldn't afford to buy with cash, shed an existing

$1,100 mortgage payment, avoid a *new* mortgage payment, and add over $55,000 to her retirement nest egg. Wow! Folks, I think it's pretty clear that the HECM for purchase is a fantastic way to buy a home in retirement.

Case study #6: How a reverse mortgage helped hold one couple over until Medicare started

Let me introduce Tim and Brenda, who live in the beautiful state of Washington. Tim, 63, has his own car restoration business. Brenda, 62, does bookkeeping part-time on the side. Tim and Brenda enjoy their jobs, make a decent income, and live a comfortable lifestyle. However, Tim has had some health issues in recent years and wants to retire. He's just not physically able to do the hard work and long hours he's done in the past. His goal is to gradually wind down the business and retire completely in about 4 or 5 years.

The roadblock to retirement, however, is health insurance. Tim and Brenda are both self-employed, so they're 100% responsible for their health insurance premiums, which are a whopping $1,435 every month. Their take-home income averages about $6,000 per month, which means health insurance eats up nearly a quarter of their net income.

On top of that, they have a mortgage payment of $573.74 (principal and interest) for a 15-year fixed mortgage. They've made great progress paying down the mortgage, but it won't be paid off for another 5 ½ years.

Before we proceed further, let's check out Tim and Brenda's current cash flow situation, which can be seen in Figure 1.

Case Studies

Income and Expenses

Income	Expenses	Cash Flow
$6,000	-$5,455	$545

Figure 1. Tim and Brenda's monthly income, expenses, and cash flow.

As you can see, Tim and Brenda only have $545 left over at the end of the month. With the vast majority of their income coming from Tim's business, there's no way he can begin winding down the business and still have enough money to cover their expenses.

Tim has considered taking Social Security right now for extra income, but he wants to put that off until he's older to take advantage of a higher payout. He figures he'll still be making money from his business for a while, so it doesn't make sense to take Social Security now. He prefers to wait until the business is nearly closed.

Tim and Brenda have built up a nice net worth over the years, which is broken down in Figure 2, below. They have modest balances on the mortgage, a few credit cards, and a car loan. Their IRAs total $174,000 and they have considerable equity in their home, which is worth $420,000. Their total net worth is $558,319.

Case Studies

Balance Sheet and Net Worth

Assets	Asset Value	Liabilities	Balance
Real Estate	$420,000	Mortgage	$34,381
Checking/Savings	$4,000	Credit Cards	$1,500
Retirement Accounts	$174,000	Auto Loans	$3,800
Total Assets	$598,000	Total Liabilities	$39,681
		Net Worth	$558,319

Figure 2. The couple's balance sheet and net worth.

The couple considered taking income from their IRAs to cover health insurance while Tim winds down the business, but they're well aware that people live much longer these days. They don't want to start draining their IRAs too early.

If Tim is to start winding down his business, they need another way to pay for their health insurance premiums until Medicare kicks in. Fortunately, Tim and Brenda have a savvy financial adviser who is very familiar with reverse mortgages. He recommends they use the reverse mortgage as a stopgap to pay for their health insurance until Tim is old enough to qualify for Medicare. The plan is to draw income from the reverse mortgage until Medicare kicks in, then convert the remaining money in the reverse mortgage to a line of credit that can be tapped as needed.

Tim and Brenda contact a lender recommended by their financial adviser and learn that they qualify for a total principal limit of $222,600. After paying off their existing mortgage and the closing costs, they have a net principal limit of $172,819 that can be used to supplement their income. Figure 3 shows the reverse mortgage breakdown.

Reverse Mortgage Summary

Payoffs and Costs		Interest Rates	
Principal Limit (PL)	$222,600	Initial Interest Rate (IIR)	3.29%
Mortgage Payoff	-$34,381	Annual MIP	0.50%
IMIP	-$8,400	**Total Interest Rate**	**3.79%**
Origination	-$4,200		
3rd Party Costs	-$2,800		
Lender Credit	$0		
Net Principal Limit	**$172,819**		

Figure 3. A breakdown of Tim and Brenda's reverse mortgage, including principal limit, closing costs, mortgage payoff, and interest rates.

Tim and Brenda opt for a 20-year term income plan, which yields them an additional $964 every month. Between the added income and eliminating the mortgage payment, they have an additional $1,538 to play with every month—more than enough to cover their health insurance premiums.

Tim and Brenda plan to use the term income for no more than 5 years, then contact their lender and convert the term income into a line of credit. All it takes to restructure their reverse mortgage is a phone call to their lender and a $20 administrative fee. Based on the projections provided by their lender, they likely will have a line of credit worth around $150,000 at the 5-year mark.

Between that and their IRAs, they'll have about $325,000 in liquid assets they can draw on for income or unexpected expenses in the future.

Tim and Brenda are particularly impressed by the guaranteed growth of the line of credit. Their IRAs have been through a few bull and bear markets over the years and it's reassuring that the line of credit comes with a guaranteed growth rate. Assuming they don't need to tap into it, the line of credit will grow from $150,000 five years from now to around $200,000 by the time Tim hits age 75. Even if they do need to draw on the line of credit, whatever remains will continue to grow with no limit as long as at least one of them lives in the home and pays the required property charges.

Tim and Brenda are really excited by what the reverse mortgage offers. Tim has been stressed out about how they are going to pay for their health insurance in the coming years. He still works hard, but his health won't allow him to work the hours he used to. Thanks to the reverse mortgage, Tim can begin winding down the business and Brenda can worry less about his health.

The added bonus is that the reverse mortgage will also provide an additional retirement asset they can live on in the future. No longer will they have to live on just Social Security and their IRAs. They will have the growing line of credit as well, which will help preserve their lifestyle, assets, and financial security for longer.

Case study #7: How a reverse mortgage saved a former music teacher from unpayable credit card debt

Peggy is a 72-year old widow who loves her modest lifestyle in the beautiful mountains of western North Carolina. A former music teacher, Peggy has been retired for 7 years, but still gives piano lessons on the side to supplement her pension and Social Security income.

Peggy's budget has always been tight, but she lived comfortably until a year ago when she was hit with some big unexpected expenses. With little savings, Peggy was forced to borrow on her credit cards to pay for medical bills, a new roof, and a new water heater. Peggy admits that a good chunk of her credit card debt was from a few splurges she couldn't really afford as well, but most of it was from the financial emergencies.

Today, Peggy has $32,000 in credit card debt and it takes almost every last penny of her income to pay just the minimum payments of $600 per month. She's making little to no headway on the balances.

On top of that, Peggy has a small 30-year fixed mortgage she took out just after she retired to remodel her kitchen and bathrooms. Today, she owes $44,439 on the mortgage and has about 23 years left before it's paid off. The mortgage payment is just $276.10, but even that has become a burden.

Before we proceed further, let's summarize Peggy's current cash flow situation in Figure 1, below.

Case Studies

Income and Expenses

Income	Expenses	Cash Flow
$3,165	-$3,042	$123

Figure 1. Peggy's monthly income, expenses, and cash flow.

As you can see, Peggy only has $123 left over at the end of the month once her *regular* monthly expenses are paid. This is all she has left to set aside for "one off" expenses throughout the year like oil changes, property taxes, and insurance premiums. She's running so tight that she's had to charge such expenses on her credit cards, which isn't sustainable over the long term.

It's obvious Peggy won't be paying off her credit cards anytime soon the way things are going. So much of her minimum payments are going to interest that she's making little to no headway on the balances. It's going to take 20 years to pay off the credit cards at the rate she's going. And what happens if she has another financial emergency? She has almost no savings and her credit cards are nearly maxed out.

Before we proceed further, let's check out Peggy's balance sheet, which is shown in Figure 2. As you can see, Peggy has very little liquid cash to pay for unexpected expenses. She's also very heavy on debt, which leaves her with almost no cash at the end of the month to build up her savings or make extra payments to pay off her debt. Peggy's budget is effectively "redlined", which means she's one financial emergency away from disaster.

Case Studies

Balance Sheet and Net Worth

Assets	Asset Value	Liabilities	Balance
Real Estate	$250,000	Mortgage	$44,439
Checking/Savings	$300	Credit Cards	$32,000
Retirement Accounts	$0	Auto Loans	$0
Total Assets	**$250,300**	**Total Liabilities**	**$76,439**
		Net Worth	**$173,861**

Figure 2. Peggy's balance sheet and net worth.

Fortunately, Peggy has substantial equity in her home. She's maintained her home well and it's appreciated in value to $250,000. At the recommendation of a friend, Peggy contacts a local lender about a reverse mortgage and ends up chatting with an originator named Joe.

When Joe runs a credit report on Peggy, he notices she had some late payments on her mortgage and credit cards a year ago. When he asks what happened, Peggy explains that she was in the hospital and missed some payments. She caught them up as soon as she could, but her creditors had already reported the late payments on her credit report. Her credit scores took a hit, but Joe explains that the scores themselves don't matter. The late payments *do* matter, however, but he's pretty sure he can get her loan approved anyway. Peggy has a provable one-time extenuating circumstance that led directly to the late payments.

If it wasn't for the extenuating circumstance, the underwriter would likely require a life expectancy set-aside (LESA) to pay the property taxes and insurance for the rest of Peggy's estimated life span (according to government life expectancy tables). It's great to have the taxes and insurance paid by the reverse mortgage, but a LESA would probably make the reverse mortgage unworkable. There isn't enough money available in the principal limit to set up the LESA and pay off the existing mortgage, closing costs, and credit card debt. Fortunately, Peggy has an extenuating circumstance she can document, so the LESA won't be necessary.

When Joe crunches the numbers, he determines that Peggy qualifies for a principal limit of $148,750. After paying off her mortgage and the closing costs, she'll have $94,011 to pay off her credit cards and set up a line of credit that can be used as reserve "savings" for the future.

Because of the 60% rule, Peggy won't have access to the full $94,011 at closing. Remember, when the mandatory obligations (mortgage payoffs and closing costs, in this case) are *less* than 60% of the principal limit, you have access *up to* 60% of the principal limit in the first year. The remaining portion of the principal limit comes available at the one-year anniversary of the loan.

In Peggy's case, 60% of the principal limit equals $89,250, which is just enough to pay off the mortgage ($44,439), closing costs ($10,300), credit card debt ($32,000), and leave $2,511 available in the line of credit. The remaining $59,500 portion of the principal limit will come available at the one-year anniversary of the loan. Figure 3, below, breaks down Peggy's reverse mortgage.

Case Studies

Reverse Mortgage Summary

Payoffs and Costs		Interest Rates	
Principal Limit (PL)	$148,750	Initial Interest Rate (IIR)	3.29%
Mortgage Payoff	-$44,439	Annual MIP	0.50%
IMIP	-$5,000	**Total Interest Rate**	**3.79%**
Origination	-$2,500		
3rd Party Costs	-$2,800		
Lender Credit	$0		
1st Year Cash/LOC	**$34,511**		
2nd Year LOC	**$59,500**		

Figure 3. A breakdown of Peggy's reverse mortgage, including principal limit, closing costs, mortgage payoff, and interest rates.

When Joe presents the loan offer, Peggy is almost ecstatic. The reverse mortgage will get rid of her mortgage and credit card payments, which eliminates a whopping $876 from her monthly bills.

On top of that, the growing line of credit will serve as a reserve account she can tap into to pay for unexpected expenses in the future. Yes, Peggy will have to wait a year for most of the line of credit to come available, but she doesn't mind. Since she no longer has mortgage and credit card payments, she figures she can easily add a few thousand to her savings in the next few months. That's good enough until the remainder of the principal limit comes available in a year.

The reverse mortgage proved to be a game changer for Peggy. It rescued her from almost unpayable credit card debt, eliminated her mortgage payment, and offered a healthy reserve she can dip into for unexpected expenses. For the first time in at least a year, Peggy can rest easy at night and no longer worry about money.

Case study #8: How one man's "cash in" reverse mortgage enabled him to retire

Phil is a 67-year old mid-level manager working for a large financial services firm in Las Vegas, Nevada. Phil likes his job and his colleagues, but he's been with the company for 23 years and is ready to retire. Many former colleagues his age are already retired, so he's eager to call it quits and start spending more time on the golf course.

Fortunately, Phil's company recently offered a retirement buyout package for older workers. Phil qualifies, and he fully intends to accept the offer. His plan is to invest the buyout proceeds and some other cash he has into an annuity. According to his financial adviser, Phil can expect to receive $1,020 from the annuity every month for the rest of his life. Combined with his expected Social Security income of $2,150, Phil's total monthly income will be $3,170.

Phil could easily live on $3,170 per month if it wasn't for his mortgage. His mortgage principal and interest payment is $1,671.11 and he has 19 years to go before it's paid off. To make ends meet, Phil would have to draw money from his IRA every month, which he does not want to do. He wants to leave the IRA completely untouched until he has to start taking required minimum distributions.

Before proceeding further, let's check out what Phil's cash flow situation would look like once he retires.

Case Studies

Income and Expenses

Income	Expenses	Cash Flow
$3,170	-$3,733	-$563

Figure 1. Phil's monthly income, expenses, and cash flow.

As you can see in Figure 1, Phil would be negative $563 every month if he retired now. The mortgage payment would eat up over half his income, which doesn't leave much for other living expenses and fun activities. If Phil didn't have a mortgage payment, he could easily live on his retirement income.

Let's check out Phil's balance sheet, which is shown in Figure 2.

Case Studies

Balance Sheet and Net Worth

Assets	Asset Value	Liabilities	Balance
Real Estate	$400,000	Mortgage	$242,555
Checking/Savings	$73,000	Credit Cards	$3,400
Retirement Accounts	$232,000	Auto Loans	$4,852
Total Assets	$705,000	Total Liabilities	$250,807
		Net Worth	$454,193

Figure 2. Phil's balance sheet and net worth.

As you can see, Phil has built up a nice net worth. He bought his home a little over ten years ago when home values were much lower than today. Thanks to a hot Las Vegas real estate market, it has since appreciated to a current value of $400,000. Phil also has a good-sized nest egg in savings, though part of it is allocated to fund the annuity.

Phil's IRA has a balance of $232,000 and has performed well thanks to a booming stock market over the last decade. Again, Phil wants to use the IRA only for emergencies. He's hoping he can leave it completely untouched until he's forced to start taking required minimum distributions.

Phil has a nice net worth, but his cash flow is a problem. It's clear that the mortgage payment will prevent him from enjoying the retirement lifestyle he desires.

Phil happens to see a TV commercial for a reverse mortgage and decides to check into it. He's heard about reverse mortgages before, but he's wary because he's heard nothing but negative things about them. He's heard all the rumors about how the bank (supposedly) takes your house or steals all your equity or something. The rumors have always seemed a little overblown, so he decides to keep an open mind and hear what the lender has to say.

After crunching the numbers, Phil's originator Josie gives him some good news and some bad news. The good news is that Phil appears to be eligible for a reverse mortgage. The bad news is he's "short to close", which means he'll need to bring cash to the closing table to complete the transaction. Based on his age and home value, Phil qualifies for a principal limit of $224,800. Unfortunately, this isn't enough to cover his mortgage balance of $242,555 plus closing costs. He's short by $32,555! Ouch!

Fortunately, because Phil is starting off with a large loan balance, he's able to negotiate a lender credit of $12,000 to cover most of the closing costs. That definitely helps, but it still leaves him short by $20,555. Figure 3 shows a break down of the figures.

Reverse Mortgage Summary

Payoffs and Costs		Interest Rates	
Principal Limit (PL)	$224,800	Initial Interest Rate (IIR)	3.49%
Mortgage Payoff	-$242,555	Annual MIP	0.50%
IMIP	-$8,000	**Total Interest Rate**	**3.99%**
Origination	-$4,000		
3rd Party Costs	-$2,800		
Lender Credit	$12,000		
Net Principal Limit	**-$20,555**		

Figure 3. A breakdown of Phil's reverse mortgage, including principal limit, closing costs, mortgage payoff, and interest rates. As you can, Phil is short-to-close by $20,555.

Phil would prefer not to bring cash to closing, but it takes him only a few minutes to make his decision. He decides to pull the money out of his traditional IRA to cover the shortage. Yes, he doesn't want to touch his IRA and, yes, he'll get taxed on the money (traditional IRAs are taxable), but for him it's a no-brainer. The money he's taking out of the IRA is a relatively small portion of his total retirement assets. It's not like he's draining his assets dry to obtain the cash needed to close the reverse mortgage. Besides, if he retires with a mortgage payment, he'll have to draw money out of his IRA every month to cover his expenses anyway. He would essentially be draining his IRA to pay a mortgage he won't live long enough to pay off anyway. That's throwing good money after bad!

By paying $20,555 to get rid of a $1,671.11 mortgage payment, Phil is essentially earning an almost 100% cash-on-cash return in just the first year of the reverse mortgage. He's spending $20,555 to pay down his existing mortgage and get the reverse mortgage, but he's saving $20,053 in mortgage payments every year for potentially the rest of his life. To him, it makes perfect sense to plunk down the cash needed to close the reverse mortgage.

Phil isn't thrilled about taking $20K from his IRA, but he's ecstatic about finally retiring. To him, it's money well spent. Getting rid of the mortgage payment will make it possible to live the retirement lifestyle he's worked so hard to earn. Phil looks forward to hitting the links and spending more time volunteering for a local non profit.

Glossary

Appraisal

An appraisal is an opinion of a home's market value developed by a licensed real estate appraiser for purposes of obtaining a mortgage. The appraised value is used to determine the maximum claim amount, which is used to calculate the principal limit for a HECM reverse mortgage.

Caps

Caps are limits placed on the movement of the variable-rate HECM initial interest rate. Caps allow the initial interest rate to increase, but only within certain limits at each rate change and over the life of the loan.

Closing costs

Closing costs cover the services necessary to complete a reverse mortgage. Closing costs come in three categories: IMIP, origination, and third-party costs.

Expected interest rate (EIR)

The expected interest rate is an interest rate value used (along with the age of the youngest borrower or non-borrowing spouse) solely to determine the correct principal limit factor and calculate the initial proceeds.

Federal Housing Administration (FHA)

The Federal Housing Administration (FHA) is an agency of the United States federal government that was created under the National Housing Act of 1934. The FHA insures and regulates HECM reverse mortgages under the authority of the Department of Housing and Urban Development (HUD).

Financial assessment

Financial assessment encompasses a broad set of HECM qualifying guidelines rolled out by HUD in 2014 to address a growing default problem. Financial assessment is designed to determine if applicants have a demonstrated willingness and adequate financial resources to pay the required property charges.

Index

The index is a base interest rate used to calculate the initial interest rate for a variable-rate HECM over time. The fully-indexed initial interest rate is composed of the index plus a margin set by the lender. For example, if the index is 0.50% and the margin is 2.50%, the fully-indexed initial interest rate is 3.0%. If the index increases, the initial interest rate increases as well. The most commonly used indices for the variable-rate HECM are the 1-Month CMT and the 1-Year CMT. The initial interest rate for the fixed-rate HECM does not have an index because the rate is fixed for the life of the loan. An index (plus a margin set by the lender) is also used to calculate the expected interest rate for both the variable-rate HECM and the fixed-rate HECM. The expected interest rate is used solely to calculate initial proceeds.

Initial interest rate (IIR)

The initial interest rate is the actual note rate for a HECM reverse mortgage. The initial interest rate is composed of an index plus a margin set by the lender. For example, if the index is 0.50% and the margin is 2.50%, the fully-indexed initial interest rate is 3.0%. If the index increases, the initial interest rate increases as well. The most commonly used indices for the variable-rate HECM are the 1-Month CMT and the 1-Year CMT .

Life expectancy set-aside (LESA)

The life expectancy set-aside, or LESA, was introduced as part of the financial assessment guidelines rolled out by HUD in 2014. The LESA is designed to ensure that property taxes and homeowners insurance are paid on behalf of borrowers with damaged credit or limited income. The LESA reserves a chunk of the principal limit solely for the payment of property taxes and insurance. The exact amount of the LESA varies widely from borrower to borrower because it is based on age and the cost of property taxes and insurance.

Lender credit

A lender credit is a payment to you by the lender at closing for purposes of covering closing costs. Lenders don't waive or remove closing costs, they offset them with a lender credit. If you have a large starting loan balance (such as when you're paying off a large existing mortgage), lenders have more leeway to offer a lender credit. If your starting balance is small, the lender may not be able to offer a lender credit.

Lending limit

The FHA lending limit effectively caps the appraised value for purposes of calculating proceeds. Proceeds are calculated based on the maximum claim amount, which is the lesser of the home value or the lending limit. In other words, if the home value is less than the lending limit, the maximum claim amount equals the appraised value. If the appraised value exceeds the lending limit, the maximum claim amount equals the lending limit.

Mandatory obligations

Mandatory obligations are expenses that must be paid at closing to complete a HECM reverse mortgage. The most common mandatory obligations include existing mortgage balances, closing costs, set-asides, and property charges due at closing.

Margin

The margin is a value set by the lender and is used to calculate the fully-indexed initial interest rate. The initial interest rate is the actual note rate for a HECM. For example, if the index is 0.50% and the margin is 2.50%, the fully-indexed initial interest rate is 3.0%. A margin is also used to calculate the expected interest rate, which is used solely to calculate proceeds.

Maturity event

A maturity event causes the HECM to become due and payable in full. Examples of maturity events include the death of the last borrower or non-borrowing spouse, failing to pay the required property charges, selling the home, permanently moving out of the home, or failing to maintain the home at least reasonably well.

Maximum claim amount (MCA)

The maximum claim amount equals either the appraised value or the lending limit, whichever is less. For example, if the value of the home is $300,000, which is less than the lending limit, the maximum claim amount equals $300,000. If the home value exceeds the lending limit, the maximum claim amount equals the lending limit. The maximum claim amount is used to calculate initial proceeds.

Mortgage insurance premium (MIP)

Annual mortgage insurance premium (MIP) is assessed by FHA to insure the HECM reverse mortgage. Annual MIP is calculated like interest and accrues onto the loan balance over time. MIP (along with IMIP) makes it possible for the HECM to be a non recourse loan.

Modified tenure

A modified tenure plan is the combination of a line of credit and a lifetime tenure payout plan. Tenure or modified tenure plans are only available on the variable-rate HECM.

Modified term

A modified term plan is the combination of a line of credit and a term payout plan. Term or modified term plans are only available on the variable-rate HECM.

Non-borrowing spouse (NBS)

A non-borrowing spouse (NBS) is a spouse who doesn't qualify to be a full borrower on a HECM because they are not yet 62. Though they are not full borrowers, they inherit the protections built into the reverse mortgage if the older spouse passes away. If the older spouse dies, the non-borrowing spouse can remain living in the home without having to pay back the reverse mortgage as long as they maintain the home and pay the required property charges. The non-borrowing spouse does not retain access to any remaining funds in the reverse mortgage after the older spouse dies.

Non recourse

The HECM reverse mortgage is a non recourse loan. The most that will ever have to be repaid is the value of the home, even if the home is worth less than the loan balance. Any shortage is paid by FHA's Mutual Mortgage Insurance Fund.

Originator

An originator is the licensed professional who will be your main point of contact throughout the process of submitting and processing your reverse mortgage application. Originators are also commonly referred to as loan officers or reverse mortgage professionals.

Principal limit (PL)

The principal limit is the total gross proceeds available through a HECM *before* paying mandatory obligations like mortgages, closing costs, set asides, etc.

Principal limit factor (PLF)

A principal limit factor is a percentage value determined based on the age of the youngest borrower (or non-borrowing spouse) and the expected interest rate. The principal limit factor is derived from a table published by HUD and is multiplied by the maximum claim amount to determine the principal limit.

Processor

A processor is a professional who will help complete your reverse mortgage once the underwriter has issued a conditional loan approval. The processor and originator could be the same person if you're working with a small lender. If you're working with a large lender, the processor will likely be a different person than your originator.

Property charges

Property charges include property taxes, homeowner's insurance, flood insurance, homeowner's association (HOA) dues, ground rents, and special assessments, where applicable. A failure to pay the required property charges could trigger a maturity event and make the HECM due and payable.

Repair set-aside

A repair set-aside reserves a portion of the proceeds from a HECM to ensure required repairs are completed after loan closing. Once the repairs are completed, the funds in the repair set-aside are released back to the borrower.

Servicing fee

Some lenders charge a monthly servicing fee throughout the life of the reverse mortgage to cover ongoing customer service expenses. Lenders are required to disclose any servicing fees during the application process. Servicing fees are less common today, but they're usually around $30/month for lenders that still charge them. You do not need to pay servicing fees out of pocket. They're simply added to the loan balance over time.

Tenure

A tenure plan offers monthly income guaranteed for life, regardless of how long you live. Because tenure income comes with a lifetime guarantee, it's often lower than what you might receive with a term payout plan. Tenure payments are calculated assuming you'll live to age 99, but they're guaranteed to continue if you live longer or use up all of the equity in your home. Tenure payments are only available on the variable-rate HECM.

Term

A term plan offers income for a certain period of time or payment amount. Unlike tenure, term payments do not come with a lifetime guarantee, so there is a risk they could run out at some point. Because there is no lifetime guarantee, term payments are often higher than tenure payments. Term payments are only available on the variable-rate HECM.

Notes

1. U.S. Census. (2015). *Wealth and Asset Ownership for Households, By Type of Asset and Selected Characteristics.* Retrieved from https://www2.census.gov/pr ograms-surveys/demo/tables/ wealth/2015/ wealth-asset-ownership/wealt h_tables_cy2015.xlsx

2. U.S. Senate Special Committee on Aging. (1969, July 31). *Economics of Aging: Toward a Full Share in Abundance.* Retrieved from https://www.aging.senate.g ov/ imo/media/doc/publications/7311969.pdf

3. U.S. Department of Housing and Urban Development. (2020, February 29). *HECM Endorsement Summary Report February 1, 2020 to February 29, 2020.* Retrieved from https://apps. hud.gov/pub/chums/f17fvc/hecm.cfm

4. Brookings Institution (2019, October). *Unlocking housing wealth for older Americans: Strategies to improve reverse mortgages.* Retrieved from https://ww w.brookings.edu/wp-content/uploads/2019/10/ES_20191016_MoultonHau rin_ReverseMortgages.pdf

5. U.S. Department of Housing and Urban Development. (2017, August 29). *HECM Principal Limit Factor Tables—Effective October 2, 2017.* Retrieved from https://www.hud.gov/ sites/dfiles/SFH/documents/PLF_on_after_10_2_17. xls

Acknowledgments

I'm deeply indebted to my lovely wife, who has offered boundless support and encouragement through the ups and downs of the mortgage industry and the process of writing this book. I love her so much and she truly helps me be a better human being.

I would like to thank my Dad for his support and proofing for this project. A writer himself, I deeply respect and value his opinions and feedback.

I'm also indebted to the trainers, coaches, and colleagues who helped me over the years to grow into a successful mortgage professional. Their influence and impact is woven deeply throughout this book.

Finally, I thank my Creator, the Father of lights, who has given me so much to be thankful for. I'm far from perfect, but I wouldn't be the man, husband, or father I am today without the grace and goodness He has shown me.

About the Author

Mike Roberts is an author, blogger, and financial services professional with more than fifteen years of experience in the mortgage lending industry. He has helped hundreds of seniors over the years obtain reverse mortgages and enjoy a more financially secure retirement. Mike Roberts is the founder of MyHECM.com, a leading free online resource for seniors, their families, and their advisers to learn more about the HECM reverse mortgage. Mike enjoys spending his time with his lovely wife and their three children. He also loves to ski, hike, surf, or read a good book with a cool brown ale or a hot cup of coffee.

Please visit https://www.myhecm.com or follow Mike Roberts on Twitter at @myhecm.

You can connect with me on:
🌐 https://www.myhecm.com
🐦 https://twitter.com/myhecm

www.ingramcontent.com/pod-product-compliance
Lightning Source LLC
Chambersburg PA
CBHW071000261225
37339CB00021B/295